*The Affair of
Gabrielle Russier*

The Affair of
Gabrielle Russier

with a Preface by Raymond Jean

and an Introduction by

MAVIS GALLANT

The letters and M. Jean's preface

translated from the French by

Ghislaine Boulanger

 Alfred A. Knopf   New York   1971

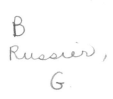

THIS IS A BORZOI BOOK
PUBLISHED BY ALFRED A. KNOPF, INC.

Copyright © 1971 by Alfred A. Knopf, Inc.
Introduction Copyright © 1971 by Mavis Gallant

All rights reserved under International and Pan-American Copyright Conventions. Published in the United States by Alfred A. Knopf, Inc., New York, and simultaneously in Canada by Random House of Canada Limited, Toronto. Distributed by Random House, Inc., New York. Originally published in France as *Lettres de Prison* by Éditions du Seuil Paris. Copyright © 1970 by Éditions du Seuil.
ISBN: 0–394–46924–0
Library of Congress Catalog Card Number: 75–154931
The Introduction by Mavis Gallant was printed in *The New Yorker* magazine.
Manufactured in the United States of America

FIRST AMERICAN EDITION

*Condamnée le 10 juillet dernier à douze mois de
prison avec sursis et à 500 F d'amende pour détournement de mineur, Mme Gabrielle Russier,
trente-deux ans, professeur de lettres, a été trouvée
morte, lundi soir, dans son appartement marseillais de la Résidence Nord: elle s'était suicidée en
s'intoxiquant par le gaz. L'aventure vécue durant
plusieurs mois par la jeune femme avec l'un de ses
jeunes élèves trouve ainsi un épilogue tragique.*

—Le Monde, 4 *septembre* 1969

Contents

Things Overlooked
Before

*"If she had been a hairdresser,
or if she had slept with a young apprentice,
it would have been different."*
                        —THE DEPUTY PUBLIC PROSECUTOR

To translate the Gabrielle Russier case into American terms you would have to improvise a new society. First, every teacher and professor in the country, from kindergarten on through university, would be a federal employee, like the tax inspector or the postman, with a civil service career controlled, observed, and directed from Washington. This society would have such a tight cultural unity that in every region and in all walks of life words and expressions would have the same meaning, the same resonance: a doctor in Oregon, an unemployed laborer in Buffalo, a librarian in Los Angeles, and a waitress in New York could respond in much the same way to "the child," "the father," "a teacher," "the family," "a divorced woman," "an educated person," and "authority." Given this background, imagine that somewhere in the South a high school teacher of thirty falls in love with one of her pupils, a boy of seventeen. The boy's parents are both university professors. When they discover the affair, they lodge a complaint in court for corruption of a minor.

Suppose that this charge is serious when it is leveled against a woman, but barely important if the accused is a man. The reason would be not only a long history of American jurisprudence, but a prevailing belief that a Don Juan is simply exercising a normal role in society, whereas women have been troublemakers ever since Genesis.

As for the boy in the story, an adolescent who sleeps with a woman older than himself, disobeys his parents, and runs away from home will be considered not only a social delinquent but a mental case, and treated as such.

Imagine that habeas corpus does not exist in American law, but that preventive detention does: anyone can be put in prison without a trial and kept as long as the judge conducting the preliminary investigation sees fit. This judge is sovereign. He is not obliged to consult anybody or give a reason for whatever he decides. When the teacher is arrested and held without a trial public opinion is aroused because it is utterly unusual for someone of her class and background to be jailed. If she is being treated like the illiterate and the poor then something must be wrong. All over America, people wonder what the courts are up to. Eventually she is brought to trial in secret, in a closed court, and let off with a suspended sentence. Half an hour after the sentence has been passed, the district attorney, who has received a telephone call from the Department of Health, Education and Welfare, appeals to a higher court for a stiffer penalty. The object is to make certain that the teacher will have a prison record, thus making it impossible for her to earn her living anywhere in the United States. The teacher kills herself.

4

Now you must suppose that this case could have such a hold on the public mind that all over America hardly anything else will be talked about; that anyone with access to a typewriter or a microphone—journalists, welfare officers, churchmen, political activists of all persuasions, government officials, magistrates, lawyers, psychiatrists, sociologists, leaders of parents' associations and of student movements—will make passionate statements concerning the law, morality, hypocrisy, preventive detention, discrimination against women, the rights of minors, the need for prison reform, the absurdities of the criminal code, and the abuses of power.

The boy's parents are Communists. The boy is a Maoist. Imagine that major and minor doctrinaire differences on the Left could become a subject of excited discussion in the American press, and that readers will know what it is all about and be deeply interested. (There will be virtually no news of the case on television, which is government-owned and censored from Washington.) However, the *New York Times* and the Washington *Post* will publish letters and even editorials expressing surprise that Communists could behave repressively, and reproaching the parents, both gently and violently, for having cooperated with the bourgeois police.

The teacher's death is an event of national importance. It is brought up at a televised presidential press conference. The president (a Ph.D. in literature from Yale) will quote, from memory, a poem about a girl martyred by society because she loved the wrong person. The poem is the work of a celebrated American writer, patriot, and member of the Communist party.

5

Of course it sounds hopelessly wrong; this is not an American tragedy. It needs its own context, which is custombound, authoritarian, with laws established under Napoleon and a Mediterranean tradition of paterfamilias; it needs a sheltered academic atmosphere where literature is taught as a way of life, almost as a substitute for experience. Given that particular climate, it was easy for someone like Gabrielle Russier, who was intellectually developed but emotionally very young, to become fatally mistaken about possibilities and consequences. The specific sexual situation of the young boy and the older woman is a repeated theme in French novels and plays. She knew it, because she taught Racine and Stendhal, Colette and Radiguet; she grew up in a society where books are revered, but she obviously knew nothing about what that same society would tolerate in practice. She identified herself with Phaedra and Antigone, but must have forgotten that the same Greeks who called them heroines admired only heroes in real life—a life in which women had no status, none whatever.

She was not at all like other teachers. When she walked into the Lycée Saint-Exupéry in Marseilles in October 1967 to take over three classes in French literature, troisième, seconde, and première—the equivalent of grades ten, eleven, and twelve—the students thought she was a new girl. She was thirty, but looked eighteen. She was tiny, less than five feet tall, and weighed about ninety pounds. Her hair was cropped short, as boys' hair used to be. More than one person shown a picture of her after her love affair became public property thought it was the boy in the case they were seeing, not the woman. In one of her letters she calls herself "an androgynous hippie," which is much the way people were to describe her later on. She was not pretty: her nose was too long and she had the intellectual sheep's profile that for some reason abounds in academic circles. In some photographs she looks like a young Bea Lillie, but she is a sad comedian, grave, or worried, or anxious, or severe. In others she looks like a charming boy, like a head by Piero della Francesca. No one can recall a picture of her smiling. Some people remember her eyes as green, others say no, dark brown. Her students worshiped her. They called her "Gatito," which is Spanish for "little cat," and they used the familiar *tu* in addressing her. This is so unusual from pupil to teacher in France that it just touches the implausible. Relations are formal in a lycée. Even young children would be called *vous*. (Lycées are not high schools: classes start with the equivalent of grade six—the students are about eleven years old—and go on to university level.) One of the complaints students have is that their teachers are remote as planets and that they can never discuss anything with a teacher, not even their work. Gabrielle, on the contrary, wanted to be one of them. She based much of her social life on their movies, their outings, their songs. She invited them to her apartment to talk and listen to records. The students loved this, but their parents were bothered: because she gave her students books by Jean-Paul Sartre and Boris Vian, some parents started a rumor that she was organizing a Communist cell. (She was not a

7

Communist and she was only vaguely political.) Even her car might have belonged to an adolescent. It was a small red Citroën called a Dyane, decorated with pop-art flowers, on the rear window of which she had pasted MAKE LOVE NOT WAR. Brave advice—she was a French Protestant, daughter of a respectable Parisian lawyer, granddaughter of a clergyman, and anything but an adventuress. One of her lawyers was to describe her as "a boy scout," and as a one-person welfare group, "always off to battle for just causes." To her ex-husband she was and remained "morally impeccable."

The red car was important to her; it seemed to play a role in an idea she had of herself. Sometimes she signed her letters "Dyana Rossa," meaning "red Dyane," for its color and make. At thirty, she was divorced from an engineer by the name of Michel Nogues and had custody of their nine-year-old twins, to whom she was an attentive, scrupulous, but also—to foreign eyes—a severe and unbending mother. She was half-American: her mother had come to Paris from Utah in the nineteen twenties to study music and had married a lawyer she met one night at the Opéra. Raymond Jean has written that he never heard Gabrielle speak a word of English but that he thought her American side had somehow caused her to be "different." If so, she was different on two counts: Protestants are a tight, self-protective minority in France and like all such minorities subject to legend. The myth of their supposed sexual puritanism is persistent. A foreigner of Protestant origin finds himself willy-nilly identified with a stern and dismal community, whose ideas are said to be dull and virtuous, and whose collective temperament is grim and sad. They are not expected to get much fun out of life. (Whether there is a word of truth in any of this is another matter.) Protestants are in no way put down, discriminated against, or oppressed—they are, on the contrary, frequently suspected of being behind banks and commerce and politics, all the hidden mechanisms that worry the ordinary citizen and make him feel the victim of secrets. They do tend to hang together: their home lives and their traditions are not exactly like those of the majority of the French. Gabrielle Russier's "desire to serve, in the Anglo-Saxon sense of the word," as her husband put it, may have come out of that background; it may also have accounted for the glacial discipline she imposed on Joël and Valérie, her twins, who spent most of their time in two separate rooms, like two only children. They were not allowed to leave their rooms without permission, or interrupt adults, or even be with them much. They were utterly forbidden to make "unnecessary" noise, or eat between meals, or help themselves to food when they were hungry. One of her friends later wrote that a stranger entering Gabrielle Russier's apartment would never have known there was a child in it, so profound was the hush. Her daughter, Valérie, once said to a neighbor, "My brother went out of his room without permission. He ate some jam in the kitchen. I think I had better tell my mother. She would be very angry if she knew." To some of us, nine-year-old Valérie might sound like a prig and a busybody, but as such stories are quite often repeated with the intention of gaining the listener's approval, they speak volumes about a certain idea of education.

9

Gabrielle Russier had gone back to the university of Aix-en-Provence when her children were still babies to take a degree in French literature. Part of her body of work was a paper on the use of the past tense in contemporary French fiction. With charts, graphs, and diagrams, she described how many times Robbe-Grillet or Nathalie Sarraute had employed the past absolute, the past perfect, or the imperfect when composing their novels. These studies, which are the fleas of literature, and the despair of most writers—except those of France, who rather like them—are also important elements in a university career. To Raymond Jean she had the makings of "a brilliant linguist," and there is no doubt that her progress was impressive, particularly for a young woman looking after two children. She had a government grant of about two hundred dollars a month, in exchange for which she had signed a contract binding her to teach in state schools and universities for ten years. If she had reneged on the agreement the state could have sued for the total amount of the scholarship. Actually, this seldom happens. It seems to be a soft and pleasant arrangement. There is little pressure. It can go on for years, and it explains why men and women seem to be students well into middle life—something that often puzzles Americans. She passed the competitive state examinations called the *agrégation* when she was twenty-seven, which everyone agrees is young for that particularly difficult examination. There is no equivalent for the term, or the institution, outside France; as an *agrégée*, Gabrielle Russier acquired enormous academic prestige; she could teach in a lycée or university at a salary higher than that of her colleagues, and she was embarked on a career safe from shocks and setbacks, in theory at least. An *agrégé* is supposed to know absolutely everything that has ever been written about his subject, and to know it by heart. The examinations, like so much of French education, require a prodigious memory: a candidate in geography was once failed for having forgotten the name of a Polish mountain. But *agrégés* are taught no pedagogic methods whatever, which means they usually go on teaching the way they were taught a generation earlier. After the student riots of 1968 there was talk of abolishing a system some educators consider hopelessly out of date, but the *agrégés* turned out to be a caste with a powerful voice, and the matter was dropped. Gabrielle Russier did try new methods of teaching, which may have been another reason why her pupils' parents suspected her politics. As an *agrégée* assigned to a lycée in a provincial city —Marseilles—she probably started at a salary of about three hundred and fifty dollars a month, plus a housing allowance, plus children's allowances. She was studious, hardworking, fair-minded, and persistent. She has also been called "reckless," "all of a piece," and "incapable of compromising" by people who knew her. Raymond Jean has written that Gabrielle "knew what she wanted" and had a great appetite for gaining control over other people. She was expert at setting the stage for emotional scenes and then acting in them. "The result was that life around her was often tense." Some of her qualities seem greatly attractive—her ability to see her students as people and not little parrots, for example. She was wonderfully disinterested—it would be difficult to think of her as ungenerous or mean. She was able to write, from prison, "I

11

am here surrounded by people who ruined their lives for money," with as much wonder as if she had never taught Balzac and Mauriac, and had not herself come out of one of the toughest middle classes in the Western world. But there is also a lack of humor, an absence of humorous grace even in love. Could anyone but a humorless woman have signed letters "Phèdre" and "Antigone" or compared herself to the nymph Chloë? Calling herself "Dyana Rossa" is odder still, beyond any conclusions a stranger can come to without impertinence. It is just simply not usual for a grown woman to identify herself with classical heroines or with automobiles. In one letter to a girl she had met in prison she called herself "Antigone" and Christian—the boy she loved—"Oreste." Why Orestes? Because he killed his mother? And why Antigone? Was she being the faithful daughter, or the girl who defied authority and was sentenced to death? The name "Antigone" means "in place of a mother." Was that what she was trying to say? As for Phaedra, who fell in love with her stepson and committed suicide, the choice is prophetic, frightening.

"She had the childish side of all those who study too long, who live in books," one of her lawyers said. "Her world was unreal."

For a long time the boy was known only as "Christian R." because of a law that forbids naming a minor involved with the police. However, long before her death everyone came to know he was Christian Rossi, that he had a younger sister and two brothers, that he lived in Marseilles, and that his parents were professors *agrégés* at the university of Aix-en-Provence, which is next door to Marseilles, a few minutes' drive. He was tall, heavy, "almost stout," and had longish hair and a beard, which inevitably caused him to be compared with every bearded figure in history from Christ to Castro. He was devoted heart and soul to extreme left-wing politics. At sixteen, his age when she met him, he could have easily been mistaken for a man of twenty-four. (Professor Rossi, in a long interview he gave to *Paris-Match* [February 20, 1971], says that Christian became her pupil "at fifteen and a half," and that "he had neither the maturity nor the appearance" that has been described.) He was serious and sober but had a violent temper. He was unkempt, rather untidy. Because of his appearance Gabrielle Russier called him *le métèque*, which is a pejorative term for a foreigner, and also the title of a popular song about a Wandering Jew. His father was an Italian from Piedmont, his mother a French-woman brought up in a conservative Catholic atmosphere. Both parents were Communists. To a Maoist such as Christian, a Communist is someone stuffy, retrograde, bureaucratic, and suspicious of new ideas. "The quarrel between Christian and his father was really the fight between China and Russia," someone who knew them reported. There was one point of similarity, a coincidence really, between Christian's mother and Gabrielle Russier: Madame Rossi had also been considered a brilliant student. She had been one of the youngest *agrégées* of France. She too had taught in a Marseilles lycée and had been adored by her students, who had addressed her with the familiar *tu*.

Only two people ever knew how it came about that Gabrielle Russier, discreet and prudent in her private life, given more easily to comradeship with men than romance, should have finally chosen a lover from among her students. One of the two is dead, and the other, going on twenty, is light-years away from the rebellious son of sixteen and seventeen. So that in a sense there are no witnesses. From the moment their liaison became public, however, theories abounded. It was announced that he had fallen in love with an older woman because his own mother had not given him the love he needed. Or else that at seventeen he was on the homosexual slope and Gabrielle looked like a boy. Another theory was the Phaedra story—that she had preferred the son to the father, hence the father's relentlessness. There was nothing to support this last fantasy except idiot gossip. In the weekly *Paris-Match*, a well-known writer, winner of the Goncourt prize, who had never laid eyes on either of the lovers, testified that Christian was frail and effeminate, a mother's boy, and that Gabrielle was a great Amazon of a woman— the very opposite of reality for either one. She was also criticized, in print, again by someone who had not met her, for having written to Christian, "You were the only man I ever knew." It was taken for granted there must have been something not quite normal about her to have written this to an adolescent . . . this most typical of all infatuated declarations. What no one questioned was just how this letter came to be made public. Was it stolen from Christian? Was his mail opened and read aloud at a press conference? Did he show it to a reporter? The bandying about of a remark she must have considered deeply intimate was the only thing "wrong" or "not quite normal." The question of what people see in each other still defies analysis. The mystery of what a couple *is*, exactly, is almost the only true mystery still left to us, and when we have come to the end of it there will be no more need for literature—or for love, for that matter. All anyone knows about this particular mystery is its background—the student riots of May 1968, when France was either within a breath of armed revolution or merely involved in a vast group therapy session. For a short time everyone could act his chosen role, and then the nation elected a conservative government. But for a few weeks young people lived in a fever of rage, hope, idealism, and anticipation that now seems indefinable except as a climate. No person involved with the movement slept at home, if he could help it. Christian's father occupied his faculty building at Aix-en-Provence, while Christian himself virtually lived in the Lycée Saint-Exupéry. As for Gabrielle—"dragged into politics by Christian," said one of his friends—she was either in the streets demonstrating with her students, or opening her flat to pupils who wouldn't or couldn't go home, or sitting in on endless discussions and committee meetings. (Christian has since been more explicit. He was sixteen and a half when the affair began; the events of May 1968 brought them together to some extent [*"ça nous a quand même rapprochés un peu"*] because they realized they thought in the same way about certain things. He cannot remember the exact beginning [*"Je ne sais pas . . . Ce doit être tout à fait banal"*].—Interview in *Nouvel Observateur*, March 1, 1971.) Her first date with Christian had a deadly serious and unwittingly comic side: She asked him to go to a movie with her. He said he was expected at a Maoist meeting. If she would attend the meeting with him, he would go to the movie with her, providing it was all right with his parents. He was still sixteen then. It was Gabrielle who rang the Rossis for permission. They knew each other—she had once been a student of theirs. After the movie she drove her pupil home and stayed to have a drink with his parents. About five weeks later, without ringing the parents and asking them anything, she and Christian took off for Italy. Christian's parents believed that he was hitchhiking with another boy, a classmate. That other boy did come along, but very soon felt that nobody wanted him: Gabrielle quarreled violently with him, called him "schizophrenic," and threw some of his luggage out the window of the Italian train. That same summer Christian's still-unsuspecting parents sent him to a family near Bonn so as to improve his German. Gabrielle turned up in her decorated Citroën saying she was a cousin who had been sent to fetch him home sooner than expected. They drove back to Marseilles and spent three weeks in her apartment. The Rossis, in the same city, knew nothing about it. The journey to Italy, and the clandestine August weeks, was about as much as the love affair amounted to. They were sometimes together after that, but wretchedly, furtively, harassed and spied on, in an atmosphere of tension and worry that would have tried lovers of much longer standing. (Perhaps because she foresaw some of it, she tried to lock him out of her apartment even before the trip to Italy, upon which he broke down the door.) From the end of the summer until her death exactly a year later, Christian was in hiding, or in a psychiatric clinic, or in a home for delinquents, or watched and surveyed by his relations, while she was in jail, or in a hospital, or in a convalescent home, or followed by plainclothesmen wherever she went. It is not surprising that she once cried to a friend, "I don't want to see him!" when she heard the ring at the door, or that between the time of her trial and her death, when the same friend said, "Christian still loves you," she looked blank, as if his name suggested nothing whatever.

But then, at the beginning, they wanted to live together forever. (Christian has since declared that he never intended to marry her, because marriage was against his Maoist beliefs—a declaration that is neither here nor there. A girl of fifteen can marry with her father's consent, but a male minor under the age of eighteen requires the personal permission of the president of the Republic, which is by no means automatically granted.) Wanting to live together meant that they presented the Rossis with an ultimatum: the parents had no face-saving way out. They could not close their eyes to the affair and call it sentimental education. Christian *looked* adult, but the Rossis knew he was not, and perhaps to parents no child ever can be. Even the most selfless and indulgent parents will seldom grant the right to a private life without a struggle. At the start of the autumn term, Gabrielle asked Professor Rossi for an interview. She was shattered and astonished when her former professor did not want her to "make her life over again," as the French expression has it, with his seventeen-year-old son. He lost his temper, shouted at her to leave the boy alone, and she came away sobbing. The only result of the interview was that the Rossis' home life became a hell of daily quarrels. Both father and son had violent tempers. Sometimes Christian sulked, sometimes he stormed out of the house and went either to Gabrielle or to family friends for a few days. According to his father, this business of sulking and disappearing for days began before the fatal interview between Professor Rossi and Gabrielle. *"Le lendemain de cette entrevue"* Christian went to school as usual, but did not return home *"ni ce soir-là ni les jours suivants."* He wrote a letter to his parents breaking off relations with them, which of course he was not in a position to do, as a minor. The parents must have taken this to heart because it became an element in the court case. The verdict in the Russier case includes this paragraph: *"Que le lendemain le jeune Rossi quittait le domicile paternel et se rendait chez la prévenue; qui'il envoyait à ses parents une lettre de rupture."* The Rossis still had no real idea of how far the affair had developed. They told their friends that the boy was "bewitched" and "under a spell" and they took him to a doctor. It was a mutual acquaintance in whom Gabrielle had confided who finally told them about Italy and the departure from Germany with a "cousin." Whether you are a lenient parent or a tyrant, it is insulting to be lied to. They thought that Gabrielle was neurotic and dangerous, a sorceress who had obtained ascendancy over an emotional boy. They also saw the affair in terms of a possible precocious fatherhood and a hampered life. When Gabrielle Russier asked if she could talk to him, Professor Rossi is supposed to have said, "My God, what does she want? Is she pregnant?" His parents were not reassured by her promise that she would see to it that Christian passed his exams: it sounded as if she wanted to take over his upbringing. Gabrielle was in love, and she was sometimes Phaedra, which means "bringer of light," and sometimes Antigone, but the Rossis saw a divorced woman with two children at home; they saw confusion, scandal, and emotional disaster.

As soon as she realized that the Rossis were seriously opposed to the affair and would on no account let Christian come and live with her, Gabrielle Russier suffered what we call loosely a nervous breakdown. She was seized with fits of uncontrollable trembling. She could not speak to anyone above a whisper. She could not stop talking about her affair with Christian and the Rossis' reaction to it. At the start of the new term she asked for three months' sick leave with pay, which she later prolonged. She was on leave with pay from early October 1968 to early April 1969. Such a long leave is unusual. She was too upset to face a classroom. It is extraordinary that it should have been she, the adult of the pair, who collapsed at the very first obstacle they encountered—a parental rebuff that any grown person might have predicted. It was almost as if at the age of thirty-one she had heard her first "no." The Rossis' next step was equally predictable: they packed Christian off to a boarding school away from Marseilles, at Argelès-Gazost, in the Pyrenees. If Gabrielle Russier lived more in books than in real life, Professor Rossi, on the contrary, had forgotten one of the lessons of literature, and that is the hopeless folly of trying to separate lovers by force. Christian loathed his new school. Gabrielle, who came to see him secretly, wrote a friend, "You wouldn't recognize him, thin, anxious, he hardly knows how to smile any more." Meeting outside the school, they were found embracing in her car and taken to a police station. It must have been thought serious, for Christian wrote, "They want to put me in a reformatory."

Affairs between teachers and students are more frequent than any of this might make it appear; if they are discreet, no one takes them seriously. The Ministry of National Education now made a move to impose discretion: Gabrielle was offered a post at the University of Rennes, at the other end of France. (Although she had no intention of accepting this post, she sent Christian a telegram about it, written in Italian and signed with a man's name—this was to get past the school censor, in case his mail was stopped. It was after receiving this telegram that he ran away. In the verdict at her trial one finds this: "she then harassed him with letters, and did not hesitate to torment the young man by letting him know about her nomination to Rennes.") Although it was a promotion from lycée to university, she turned it down. Christian was also showing the symptoms of nervous collapse: he had to be put in the school infirmary and given tranquilizers. So far his relegation to this school had produced nothing but more tumult and discord, and in November he added to it by running away. He arrived in Marseilles with toothpaste rubbed in his hair, which was supposed to make him look elderly and serve as a disguise. His parents had no idea where he was—he had last been heard of in the school infirmary under sedation. He was not with Gabrielle; she had hidden him with friends. A runaway minor is a legal matter in most countries. In France, an adult who abets him can be jailed. As the daughter of a lawyer, and a teacher of minors, she certainly knew it. One wonders what either of them meant to do next: did they think they could hide Christian until he was twenty-one? What she probably never did expect was that the Rossis would take the problem to court. No one expected it. The interest and the astonishment of French public opinion showed how unusual the case seemed to be.

The Napoleonic code does not speak of corruption of minors as such. The word used is *détournement*, which means "diversion," "deviation," "turning away." *Détournement de fonds* is how embezzlement is described, for instance. *Détournement de mineur* specifically means having caused a minor to leave home. Nothing said or written about the case ever made this clear. Most people thought and probably still think that Gabrielle Russier was charged with having slept with a boy, or that she had been sued by the Rossis. Actually, their complaint was against "X," or John Doe. Under French law, anyone who "by fraud or violence" removes a minor "from the place where he has been put by those in authority over him" can be given a sentence of five to ten years. If no "fraud or violence" was involved, the sentence can be two to five years, plus a fine. If the minor dies, the penalty is death. Every crime or simple misdemeanor involving a minor is judged in terms of these articles, everything from helping a runaway, to sexual seduction, to inciting to prostitution, to kidnapping. Sometimes the law has to stand on its head: a sixteen-year-old male prostitute was once charged with contributing to the deviation of a minor, that is, of himself. Cases involving middle-class children are almost always hushed up for fear of scandal. Those that do reach the courts generally have to do with girls from the most dispossessed ranks of society—girls who are wards of the state, whose families have long been shorn of their parental rights. It is extremely rare for a woman to be charged with having "deviated" a boy. When you read the penal code, in fact, you see that there seems to be no provision for it. But if the charge *is* laid against a woman, then the law comes down heavily. She is treated more severely than if she were a man who had seduced or "deviated" a girl. One of Gabrielle Russier's lawyers, Maître Naud, has tried to show this difference by describing a similar case: "The dean of a university faculty seduced one of his students, a girl of seventeen. There was more than thirty years' difference in their ages. They traveled together and stayed in hotels, where she used his wife's name. They exchanged passionate letters which the wife was able to intercept and so obtain a divorce. It never occurred to anybody that deviation of a minor had taken place, though the girl was only seventeen and the dean fifty. No prosecutor, no magistrate, not even the girl's family mentioned this aspect of the case. Yet if the dean had been a woman, and the girl had been a boy, a charge would have been laid at once." Nearly every person who wrote about the Russier affair, even commentators who thought she had behaved foolishly, mentioned this curious twist in the jurisprudence concerning minors. They agreed that part of her punishment came from her being a woman. It seems to be accepted that a girl of any age is asking for trouble, and should know better, while the man, the seducer, is somehow or other her victim. In fact, if a man "deviates" a girl, and the girl is fifteen or more, and if it can be shown without any ambiguity that there was mutual consent, the case is dropped. But the consent of a male minor is not taken into account, although for perfectly evident reasons it must have existed. A man's conduct is considered inevitable and therefore largely innocent, but a woman's is supposedly thought-out and reprehensible. All this is puzzling in a society where women on the whole have a better time of it than women in English-speaking countries. Frenchmen do not seem to resent women or be afraid of them, they are not bored by feminine company (all-male clubs or outings are rare and considered ridiculous), the war of the sexes scarcely exists. Equal pay for equal work is the law of the country, and women often hold more important jobs than do women in America. A woman's intelligence is respected, her professional status accepted, and as to her personal life, the French are notorious for an indifference to others that is also a form of minding one's business. But that is the swim of life, its ordinary commerce. When you read the law and when you look closely at specific social situations you discover that women never have the last word. A woman's past as well as something called "her soul" weighs in the balance when she is being judged in court. In the summer of 1970 in Aix-en-Provence a woman was sentenced to twelve years' imprisonment on the suspicion that she had incited a man to commit murder. (The murderer received only eight years.) There was not a shred of evidence against the woman except gossip about her morals, including her having slept with a man of forty-seven "when she was only twenty-two." When she asked if it was a crime for a woman to have lovers she was told, in court, "the quantity matters." The formal accusation contained, "The recital

of her existence would have tempted the pen of a Balzac,"
and the police report included, "She seems to have sold
her soul to the devil." Her private life and her "soul" re-
placed facts, something inconceivable if a man were being
judged. Once, at the trial of a girl accused of having shot
her lover, the magistrate reproached her over her taste in
books, and announced, "I have searched through the record for your soul, but I failed to find it." All this comes
under a tradition Maître Naud has called *"la latinité,"*
the Latin attitude toward men and women. A Don Juan is
admired; perhaps God punishes him, but that is God's
affair. Whereas anyone who publicly defended Gabrielle
Russier was apt to receive a deluge of letters reminding
her defender that Gabrielle was a disgrace to womanhood,
as well as a whore, a pervert, and a nymphomaniac. Gabrielle Russier was nine before women were allowed to
vote, twenty-eight when married women could have bank
accounts, and thirty before she could legally get advice
from a doctor about contraception. She died before
women were allowed to enroll their children in kindergarten without the husband's written consent, or have a
say in where the family would live. The shocked protest
that followed this last piece of legislation was like a Victorian joke. After the Liberation, women who had slept
with Germans (prostitutes, mostly) had their hair cut
off, while men who had willingly gone to work for the
German war effort more often than not got away with it.
A woman found guilty of adultery in France can be sent
to jail for two years, whereas a man escapes with a fine—
and he can be fined only if he was stupid enough to bring
his mistress into his home. None of this is to say that if

24

women had been allowed bank accounts before 1965, Gabrielle Russier would have found tolerant magistrates, for Americans do not need to be told at this stage of their social history that you cannot legislate attitudes.

The Rossis had lodged their complaint against "X," without naming anyone. Nevertheless, the first person the judge conducting the preliminary investigation asked to see was Gabrielle. He asked her if she knew where Christian was hiding. "Find out for yourself—it's your job," she is supposed to have said, and even, "All right then, arrest me!" Talking back to any functionary "in the performance of his duties" is a misdemeanor in most Latin countries. (No similar law protects the public from the clerk in the post office, let alone someone more exalted.) The magistrate is said to have lost patience with her. (One can't help noticing that everyone connected with this case was either irritable or violent. Christian broke Gabrielle's door in, she threw a young boy's luggage out a train window, Professor Rossi had a violent temper, as did Gabrielle's ex-husband, who was said to fly into a rage if anything crossed him—in one of her letters she cautions him about this. As for members of the legal profession, they were at the end of their patience when proceedings were barely under way. Even the Ministry of Justice was to explain the case by saying that the boy's parents had begun the whole affair because they had lost patience too.) The examining judge did not waste time arguing with her. Three weeks after Christian had vanished from school, she

was charged and arrested without warning. Four men
arrived at her door, the magistrate among them. One
heard that her flat was searched from eight at night until
two in the morning, which seems unlikely, for no policeman is allowed to enter a private home between sunset
and sunrise. The search party may have been looking for
drugs as well as for Christian: there is an account of a
policeman biting an aspirin in two to see if it tasted peculiar. They also turned out all the dried herbs in her kitchen,
looking for pot. Because she kept a bottle of Scotch in the
house she was asked if she let her students drink. In her
bathroom, the four men came across "feminine articles"—
sanitary napkins, from the sound of it— and reproached her
for leaving such things where her children might see them.
At the end of the search, long after dark, she was taken away.
An examining magistrate is not required to notify anyone
of an arrest; Gabrielle was not able to get in touch with
anyone until the next day. She had not been convicted
of anything; nevertheless she was photographed and
fingerprinted and given a number exactly as if she had
been sentenced. One of her fellow prisoners said later,
"The first and worst of the humiliations was being ex-
amined entirely naked before the others. Never in her
entire life had Gabrielle felt such shame, but no one took
the slightest notice." In a textbook issued for prison
guardians, specific mention is made of the business of
stripping and searching: it is supposed to be a psychological "contest" from which "the prison authority must
emerge the victor." It is a known way of breaking morale
in all countries. The prisoner is searched coldly, efficiently,
silently, and, from his point of view, obscenely. His naked-

ness among the uniformed makes him seem inferior, help-less, and finally submissive.

How could any of this happen to someone who had been charged with a relatively simple offense, who had never been in trouble with the law, and had never been tried? The answer is the system of preventive detention. If you are arrested for questioning in France you are taken to the police, then before the examining magistrate. The only information he will have about you is a report called a "telegram." It can be a long list of facts, or a terse state-ment. The first thing the magistrate can decide, without asking you a single question, is whether to keep you under arrest or not. If you seem to be an educated person, well dressed, living at a respectable address, if the charge against you is not too serious, if you are not likely to run away, then you will most probably be let free until the case comes up. If you have no fixed domicile (perhaps you live in furnished rooms or a hotel), if you are an im-portant witness who might vanish, if you are dangerous to society—*presumed* dangerous, for at that point you have not been tried for anything, let alone judged—then you can be held as long as the magistrate thinks it neces-sary. Perhaps you are merely what Casamayor (the pseu-donym of a distinguished magistrate, and a judge of appeal, who writes about such matters) has called "just a poor devil," someone penniless and shabby, of a race instinctively considered inferior—Algerian, for example—then your fate may seem to have less meaning. You disappear into prison—no one will ever get up a committee to see what has become of you. The magistrate is not obliged to ask anyone's permis-sion or advice: his signature is all that matters. You may not even be the supposed culprit, but just a closemouthed witness. The judge suspects you know more than you intend to say. He is free to hold you until you change your mind. If you turn out to be innocent you have no recourse against the law. You cannot even sue for the symbolic one franc (twenty cents) in damages, though preventive detention may have cost you your job, your domestic equilibrium, and your reputation. When Gabrielle Russier was arrested for the first time, the public suddenly learned that a large section of the prison population was composed of persons awaiting trial, some of whom had been waiting for months.

It was at this point, in December 1968, that the story, which had circulated for weeks in university circles around Marseilles and Aix-en-Provence, became public property. A blurry picture of a tense woman who looked like a boy accompanied the first accounts of the runaway minor and the Communist parents who had not hesitated to turn to the bourgeois courts. One person in five votes for the Communist party in France, year in and year out, and so, of course, a large section of the public was directly interested. French news reporters, unless they work for government-owned radio and television stations, are allowed much more personal expression than in the English-speaking world. If Gabrielle Russier was described as a sympathetic figure who had risked all for love, or as a rebel standing up to a repressive structure, the Rossis were criticized left, right, and center. It seemed unbelievable that Communist parents could object to free love, or apply middle-class standards of behavior to their children, or make use of a capitalist law machine. Right-wing papers poked fun at them, orthodox Communist papers had hard words for the government but not the Rossis, while the liberals and the Maoists called it a betrayal. There were long, earnest, and irrelevant discussions in print as to just *how* Communist the Rossis were; whether they were good Communists or bad; what their attitude had been during the Algerian war (which had ended when Christian was ten); whether Professor Rossi was not more Maoist than he should be, and how he felt about the Italian Communist party. One writer assured everyone that the Rossis' reaction to various stands taken by the Italian Communist party had been "positive," whatever that meant. Madame Rossi was harshly dealt with. "She's fifty, but looks twice her age," was solemnly announced over the air. There were conjectures as to her motives, her attitude to her children, her character, her capacity for affection, all by persons who had usually never laid eyes on her. "A friend of the family," a woman with a strong Marseilles accent, undertook (anonymously of course) to inform millions of radio listeners that Madame Rossi was "disagreeable," "a shrew," and that she forced her husband to wash dishes. The scorn in the anonymous voice was indescribably droll. She sounded like a monologue in an old Marcel Pagnol film. "They must be making seven hundred thousand francs a month between the two of them," the family friend went on, as if this were an added grievance. "Seven hundred thousand francs" means seven thousand new francs, or about fourteen hundred dollars. (As professors *agrégés* attached to a university they might, in fact, have earned more than this.) The suggestion was that a man who earned money and yet washed dishes would be capable of anything. "He was all for sexual liberty," one also heard, "but not for his own wife and children." If the French Communist view of the bourgeoisie is like the old cartoon symbol of the capitalist with money bags in his pocket and a top hat on his head, the middle-class fantasy about Communists wallowing in pornography turns out to be just as peculiar. It takes a great stretch of imagination to envision an old-fashioned French Communist, with his earnest conversation, his crumpled, respectable suit, and his fat, comfortable wife, engaged in a sexual orgy. The Victorian primness that prevails in the Soviet Union was never mentioned. Perhaps no one had heard of it. At first the Rossis said absolutely nothing, then Christian's mother sent a dignified letter to a newspaper. She mentioned the "traumatic effect" the boy's liaison and the discussion it entailed were having on his younger sister and two younger brothers, adolescents too. But what seemed to shock and surprise the public most (and to a foreigner this was most striking of all) was that someone of Gabrielle Russier's class and background should receive the same treatment as a person illiterate or poor. One was made uneasy, finally, at the slant of some of the protest; how could they arrest a university graduate, a professor, an *agrégée*? It was, said Casamayor, "abnormal and rare," "unusual for someone of her class and for someone with a legal domicile." It was exactly this "abnormality" that led many liberals to take up her cause: preventive detention was so unaccountable in terms of her station in life that it became suspect. Why was she in jail? Had she really been arrested for having slept with a boy? Was she so dangerous to society that she had to be plucked out of it overnight? Was there more to the charge than anyone knew about? The public was reminded over and over that this was "a professor with an advanced university degree." (Later she came to dread these press campaigns, thinking they did her more harm than good, and her lawyers would finally beg her friends not to say anything on her behalf.) But here was another contradiction: the fact that she *was* a "person of quality" turned out to be one of the factors held against her. She was educated, she was a teacher, she should have known better. In other words, had she been an ignorant pauper there might have been no case, and if there had been, the Public Ministry—the department of the public prosecutor—might not have cared as much about getting a conviction. As the deputy public prosecutor was to say, later, "If she had been a hairdresser, or if she had slept with a young apprentice, it would have been different."

It was plain to anyone interested in the case, and it must have been clear to her too, that she could be free in a minute by telling where Christian was hiding. This she was unlikely to do. It was up to Christian to give himself up. Before doing so he asked for assurance that he would not be arrested too. The day after he appeared— the judge received him on a Sunday, most unusual—at the Palace of Justice (courts of law) in Marseilles, her order for release was signed. With Gabrielle free, Christian's freedom became a problem, for the two had no intention of parting, and he did not wish to live at home *or* in a boarding school. His parents took an extreme step—they asked a judge of the juvenile court to intervene. No one seemed able to decide if Christian had fallen in love with a woman of thirty-one because there was something the matter with him, or whether he had become unruly and disobedient as a result of the affair. The idea of sexual attraction, or love, or both together, appeared to be so singular that a rational explanation had to be discovered and a remedy applied. The judge ordered Christian sent to an examination center for delinquent minors, to see if he was a neurotic requiring treatment. The boy spent Christmas at the center, and was bored and miserable. After a number of tests and interviews, it was decided that he was not deranged, but had an intellectual and emotional maturity beyond his years. This is not as good as it sounds, for young persons who seem remarkably mature often have problems, or the groundwork for them. At any rate, no therapy was suggested. Still unconvinced, Christian's parents had him transferred from the center for delinquent minors to a private psychiatric clinic where a course of treatment could be applied. The guardian of a minor has the right to do whatever he thinks best, and no state psychologist or social worker would be likely to question the decision of an educated parent. In the clinic, Christian was kept alone and given tranquilizers. He had no one to talk to and nothing to do. Sometimes he was allowed out of his room and on one such occasion he managed to escape. He went straight to Gabrielle. He was very thin, and groggy from the drugs he had been given. She opened the door and burst into tears.

The charge against her was still open, but Christian had such a horror of the clinic that she was not likely to send him back there. Knowing the risk she was taking, she hid him with friends. But the friends could not keep him forever either; they got in touch with the Rossis, who now began their original procedure all over—Christian was again interviewed by a judge of the juvenile court and *again* sent to the center for delinquent minors for observation. He stayed there three weeks, idle and bored. The psychiatrists at the center did not propose any kind of treatment or therapy. He had become somebody nobody knew what to do with. At last the judge suggested sending him to a home for boys. It was not a punitive establishment, but a reeducative shelter for minors who had been in trouble with the law. Discipline was relaxed; the boys slept there but went out to work or to school. Christian, enrolled in a new lycée, discovered that Saturdays and Sundays at the shelter were free. Every Saturday and Sunday, therefore, he appeared on Gabrielle's doorstep. They made no effort to hide, but went openly to restaurants and movies and drove about Marseilles in her bright red car followed by plainclothesmen dressed as students. During this time Christian was skipping classes and vanishing from the lycée during school hours. The vice-principal of the lycée sent a note to Professor Rossi warning him that the boy might be expelled. (Christian's irregularity at school was also mentioned in the verdict.) After three weekends of this, the examining magistrate sent for Gabrielle and gave her a serious warning. He thought she did not understand the danger she was in, or that the charge against her could lead to prison. Her argument was that she loved Christian and that she had never promised not to see him, but that was no argument. Christian was also summoned for an interview at the Palace of Justice. As he was leaving the building, two men who turned out to be male nurses seized him by the arms and dragged him to an ambulance parked a few feet away. They were acting on his father's instructions, and were employed by the private psychiatric clinic from which Christian had fled earlier that winter. The walls were padded. The only lavatory was a hole in the floor. He stayed there for two months.

Perhaps it did not happen that way. Perhaps Christian went to the clinic willingly, like any patient, but afterward could not remember. On the other hand, perhaps he was dragged to an ambulance from the steps of the Palace of Justice, in Marseilles, and kept in solitary confinement, and forced to submit to a drastic form of therapy known as "the sleep cure," whether he needed it or not. Either way, voluntary or forced, medically justified or medically lunatic, it would have been *perfectly legal.* The guardians of a minor have not only the law but the full weight of public opinion behind them. Even when Christian's version of the story appeared in print it was difficult to find anyone except psychiatrists and educators who entirely disapproved of the sleep cure: the boy sounded nervous and moody, he was a chronic runaway, doctors must know what they are doing, and a long sleep never did anyone any harm. Actually, no one ever denied Christian's story. The director of the clinic observed a scrupulous professional silence and did not sue the author of an account that mentioned the clinic by name. In France, as in most countries, no doctor will ever criticize another except behind his back. No medical or psychiatric association ever asked for an investigation or even a clarification of the story, perhaps for a reason already mentioned: even if it did happen that way, it was legal.

"Put him to sleep and he will wake up cured" sounds like a fantasy, but "the sleep cure" is, in fact, a form of therapy widely used in France. Because the word "sleep" makes it sound like rest, it is often sought after by patients. It is a form of treatment that began in Austria in the early twenties, it is practiced in Switzerland, and is now something of a psychiatric fashion in France, where rest homes and clinics are equipped for administering the "cure." In serious hospital therapy it is thought to be useful when—for example—a patient is in such a state of anguish, excitement, and distress that no form of social contact at all is possible. The psychiatrist will order a sleep cure of about eight days on the average. This is supposed to break the tension and get him out of his environment. The patient either swallows or has injected large doses of tranquilizers and barbiturates in their various forms. He sleeps and dozes and is lost to the world about twenty-three hours out of twenty-four. But the cure is taken also voluntarily, eagerly, by persons who are nervous, tired, insomniac, depressed, overworked, in the midst of unhappy love affairs, or up against any of the problems that make people say, "If I could only sleep until it is all over . . ." To someone who is not a doctor this always sounds chilling, for the suppressed part of the sentence seems to be "and never wake up." The benefit of the sleep cure is that you do wake up: it seems like a harmless, temporary death. (One of the reasons why it is dispensed so lavishly in private clinics is that, like a course of weight reducing in similar institutions, it is

very expensive.) The sleep cure patient, exactly like a
failed suicide, comes back to the world physically weak-
ened, thinner, groggy, horribly depressed, lower in
finances, and unfortunately right back in the same life.
The sleep cure is moreover a known cause of melan-
cholia. The patient is warned about it, and often advised
to recover by getting a little mountain air. He then either
goes to a hotel or a rest home full of other sick persons.
The high altitude, the boredom of institutional life, the
solitude, the lack of anything interesting to discuss or of
any productive work to do, the company of other neu-
rotics give the final push and turn a temporary depression
into something agonizing. The backlash of the sleep cure
is, sometimes, suicide.

Christian's parents' reaction may seem extreme, but it
is not inexplicable. Where an American might expect a
boy of seventeen or eighteen to rebel, a French father
is taken aback. France is anything but a matriarchal society: public opinion holds a father responsible for his
children and the way they behave even after they grow
up. In Paris the only son of a middle-class family, psy-
chotic and with lower than average intelligence, murdered
a prostitute. During the trial it emerged that his father
had been making him an allowance of about two hundred
dollars a month. This might not seem an excessive sum
for a man to have given his dim-brained and unemploy-
able son, for at least it kept him from stealing, but suddenly the *father* became the accused. Tons of hate and
insult fell upon him because of the pocket money. As the
father left the court where he had just heard his son
sentenced to be beheaded, he was surrounded by a clot

of Parisian hags, jeering, cursing him, and shaking their fists. What was his crime? He had not behaved "like a father." "He was not a man." He had failed in his "paternal role," and the paternal role is expected to be authoritative. As you go south, the greater the role of the father. In spite of population shifts and industrialization and urbanization, the Roman paterfamilias still somehow prevails. The family structure is almost untouchable. The father represents family law, and law in general. As he obeys certain traditional social laws, so he is obeyed in turn by the group, which is his family. (These are not random musings but ideas put forward by members of the Mediterranean Psychiatric Association at a meeting in May 1970.) France is cut into two distinct climatic zones by the Loire River. South of the Loire, there are fewer divorces, fewer suicides, and—where the father's authority is strongest—four times *fewer* patricides. Catholicism alone can't account for it—the most important Protestant communities are in the south. Christian's father, who was Italian born, most certainly expected to be obeyed, and he had a long history of tradition to back him up. There is also the length of time French children live at home, for reasons both of custom and economics. Their studies seem to go on longer. When they go to the university it is in the home city, and it would be considered very strange if a son or daughter were to move out. Besides, where would he go? There is an unlimited housing crisis. Strict or not, French parents are closer to their children. They take their meals and their holidays together. It is extremely rare to hear a French person say that he does not like his parents. Perhaps the admission would be thought undignified, or perhaps you just accept your family whether you like them or not. The Russier case nevertheless inspired a number of French commentators to denounce family life as the cause of all her troubles, not to mention Christian's. Wilhelm Reich was quoted more than once, and there were waves of Freud, Marx, Lenin, and Engels, because of his book on the family, which became a favorite of lycée students and has remained so. No one mentioned Georg Groddeck's belief that if an element of cruelty were not present in every form of education not even the most loving mother would lift a finger to teach a child anything. Parents do the most astonishing things, all in the name of love: for in spite of everything that was said and written about the Rossis, nothing led one to believe that the Rossis did not love Christian. "What would you have done in my place?" Madame Rossi asked a reporter, who replied, "I don't know what I would have done, but I know what I *wouldn't* have done," which seems to beg the question. Even if parents are certifiably demented they don't imagine the most damaging, the most irreparably wicked, the most demonic thing they can do and then go ahead and do it: they always think it is the right thing. If you ask in whose interest, the parent will answer, "The child's," and that is the only inaccuracy. Dreadful mistakes are made for the sake of safeguarding a problematic, an imaginary future. When Christian's parents told their friends he was "bewitched" and "under a spell" they must have believed it. The modern exorcist is the psychiatrist, and so he was called in to expel the spirit that had taken possession of their son.

Christian has told a writer that he underwent two

forced sleep cures, each lasting three weeks. He dozed, drugged, round the clock, and was wakened only for meals, which he ate in a drowsy state.

At the end of the first three weeks he had an interview with his father. It was unsatisfactory, and about a week later he was subjected to a second cure. There was no public medical reaction to this account when it appeared in print, because of the known prudence of doctors, but there was plenty of professional comment in private. The treatment could not have killed him, but it might have made him very ill and, if he *was* the nervous, moody person that was suggested, it could have made him afraid of a number of things for life. However, his parents must have had a reason for committing him, and the medical director of a licensed establishment saw no harm in it: otherwise, he would have refused. One of the delusions mental patients have sometimes is that they were dragged into clinics and forced to submit to intolerable treatment. But how ill was he? He had twice been seen by state-appointed specialists who thought there was nothing the matter with him. Raymond Jean was not only a friend of Gabrielle Russier, but a friend and university colleague of Professor Rossi. Of course, wrote Raymond Jean, Christian was legally a child and had to be protected and defended against himself. But was it really protection to commit him to a home for delinquents or "to a cell in a psychiatric clinic, to deliver him over to injections and sleep cures"? At any rate, it happened and there were two results: One was that Christian acquired a horror of clinics and psychiatric treatment, that his overriding obsession to this day (he is still under twenty-one) is the fear that he might be committed to an institution by force. But that came later—the immediate result, after two months of incarceration, was that he said he would do whatever his parents liked. He agreed not to see Gabrielle again, on which he was released and sent off to live with a grandmother in another city. Again he was enrolled in a new lycée. As his health and vitality came back, he found being watched and observed and controlled utterly intolerable. Everyone seemed afraid he would break his promise and run away, and, finally, that is what he did. He got to Marseilles, went to a friend's house, and telephoned Gabrielle. He knew by then, but perhaps did not fully grasp, the meaning of the difficulties this would bring her. He understood that if he went into hiding—his intention now—she would be jailed. "Do whatever you like," she is supposed to have told him. They did not see each other. Except for one meeting in a public park, in the presence of another person, they never saw each other again. She prepared to be jailed now with such resignation, complaisance almost, that her friends were aroused. "She was highly intelligent," said one of her colleagues, "but in love she had the sentimentality of a little housemaid fresh from the country." Gabrielle said to her friends, "When I am in jail, Christian's parents will see how much I love him." One can only suppose that she had weighed all the consequences —whether her small twins needed her more than Christian needed a showdown with his parents, for instance. Valérie was at a holiday camp in the mountains. Gabrielle now arranged for her cleaning woman to look after Joël (she is the "Madame R." of the letters) and, remembering the humiliating search of her apartment that had preceded the first arrest, she gave her personal papers to a neighbor. Two days after Christian had vanished from his grandmother's, Gabrielle was committed to the Marseilles prison known as Les Baumettes.

She was arrested in April and held until mid-June, two months in all. She still had not been convicted of anything. After her death the minister of justice said that her "education" had been taken into account and that the prison authorities had tried to limit the chances of "contagion" from other prisoners. He also remarked, crossly, that he was tired of hearing about bad conditions in Les Baumettes. This prison consisted of three large blocks with barred windows, one block each for men, women, and minors. Police dogs roamed the space between buildings and lights were played on the windows at night, as if it were a top-security edifice for criminal lunatics. Although the women were as a rule four to a cell, Gabrielle was given certain privileges: she was allowed at first to share a cell with only two women, both accountants, and considered closer to her by education than prostitutes. They were, in fact, a pair of active lesbians, and she loathed the cohabitation. She was horrified by nearly all of the prisoners. For the first time in her life this extreme romantic came into contact with the by-products of poverty, prostitution, and thievery. Later, one of the other prisoners, a girl by the name of Muriel, wrote that Gabrielle was simply unable to understand or to cope with "the spitefulness, the jealousy, and the vulgarity" that prevail in the penitentiary world. "She had lost even her name. She was nothing more than number 59.264."

Prisoners were allowed out in the walled courtyard between two and four in the afternoon. When Gabrielle
first appeared in the yard none of the other women
knew anything about her. "Because her hair was cut very
short, like a boy's, the most spiteful of the prisoners put
the word around that she was a lesbian." Odious comments and remarks were made in her presence. "Gabrielle,
pale as the dead, listened without saying anything. She
resembled a frightened little girl brought face-to-face with
the ferocity of adults." In time, she learned to answer her
tormentors "gently and intelligently." She infuriated the
prison guards by her good manners, and because she never
acquired the filth or the slang of prison jargon. She was
forced to hear "revolting obscenities" addressed to her
by these same guardians, most of it about her having
slept with an adolescent. One day when Gabrielle was
reading in the prison library one of the guards said to
her, "What's the good of that to you? You're nothing but
an old rag now. Your life is finished." And yet in her
letters she says that, finally, she preferred the guards to
her fellow prisoners. Her prison friendship with Muriel
was a curious one. In a way, this girl, who was eighteen,
seems to have become a nonsexual substitute for Christian. Muriel was a heroin addict, serving a sentence for
possession of narcotics. (There was a separate block for
minors, but perhaps the nature of the charge had caused
her to be placed with older women.) Gabrielle took a
great interest in Muriel, nicknamed her "Satan," and
asked to have her as a cellmate. She immediately undertook the girl's education, drew up reading lists, accompanied her to the prison library. When they were parted,

Gabrielle wrote her letters that seem oddly intense, even given the highly keyed friendships people develop when they are shut up together: "Walls separate us, but I know you are somewhere . . ."

After Gabrielle's death, reporters found Muriel in the Marseilles bars where drugs are sold. Her throaty young voice was recorded and widely broadcast. She blamed herself for Gabrielle's death because she had never made an effort to see her. The truth was that once out of jail Muriel had probably forgotten all about her. Remorse and guilt did not prevent Muriel from peddling Gabrielle's letters around. They turned up in a women's magazine, they were read on the radio. A drug addict, especially a minor, was still something of an exotic item in France in 1969. The press attitude to Muriel became tinged with some of the sentimentality spilled over from the Russier case, once Gabrielle was dead. She was invariably described as "Muriel (or Satan), the little addict." These letters were different in tone from any others collected and published. Hearing one of them read by an actress during a radio broadcast, a listener could easily have thought it was a letter to Christian. Described as "poetic," the letters to Muriel were pedantic, flowery, romantic, and pretentious—"literary" in the worst sense of the word. Sometimes Gabrielle seemed to be addressing herself; when she spoke directly to Muriel she seemed to be composing a love letter. One felt that Gabrielle must have been terribly innocent, and that she had a great desire to be loved and needed by someone young. The actresses chosen to read *any* of her letters invariably adopted pompous Comédie Française diction thickly iced with sugar, and the real voice of the prisoner who had asked, "Why am I here and what have I done?" remained silent.

Gabrielle suffered enormously from the petty horrors of prison life. Her mail was not just read and stamped by the prison censor, but held up by the examining magistrate, who was in no hurry. Some of her letters were lost and may have fallen by mistake in some legal wastepaper basket. Letters to her daughter disappeared. A neighbor of Gabrielle's wrote the judge asking if she might visit Gabrielle in prison. Only relations are allowed to see prisoners, and Gabrielle had none in Marseilles. Her mother was an invalid, paralyzed and in a wheelchair, which meant that it was difficult for Gabrielle's elderly father to leave Paris. The judge never answered the request. If she was jaunty at first, and decided to look on her imprisonment as a new experience, she soon fell into the despair that is typical of people who really do not understand why they have been arrested. That is, although she knew that Christian had run away and that she was being held as a hostage, she did not think she had done anything *wrong*. The Dominican nuns who visited her, and whom she liked, advised her to look on herself as "a political," that is, a political prisoner. It was good advice: in the Nazi camps of the Second World War, political prisoners were less likely to slip into despair and had, apparently, a better chance of survival than people who had not done anything to provoke an arrest. (There is no other possible comparison between a camp and Les Baumettes prison, of course, and one is not attempting to equate the two.) She was also desperately hard up. There was rent to be paid, and legal fees, and income tax, and the loss of social security because she was in jail. This was a blow, because it affected her children. She had devoted friends, but it does not sound as if any of them put their hands in their pockets for her—though surely that would be the first thing an imaginative friend would think of. Nevertheless, in terms of what happens to "the humble" of France, her situation as a prisoner *was* privileged. She was only one of thousands who have been held without trial, with the law creeping along at snail's pace, and their lives ruined and broken. Until this happened to an educated Frenchwoman of good family, and for a reason the readers of popular newspapers could grasp and sympathize with— love—these other prisoners might as well have been trying to hang themselves in cells in South America. The feeling in France suddenly seemed to be, "If it can happen to her, it can happen to me," whereas what happens to the Algerian street sweeper will never affect anyone. There is absolutely no doubt that if she had been obscure and "humble" she would never have been heard of and there would never have been an editorial on the front page of *Le Figaro*. One year before her first arrest, Algerian prisoners had rioted in the Santé prison in Paris. It turned out that there were twenty-seven hundred "North Africans and other foreigners" in cells each of which had only one small window just under the ceiling, and as sole sanitary installation "a water closet without a seat, the bowl of which had to serve as a sink for washing their dishes and as a washbasin for their ablutions" (*Le Monde*). When, during a heat wave, these conditions became intolerable, the prisoners began a hunger strike, of which no one took the least notice. Then they began singing and banging on the doors and throwing things out the windows. In the confusion that resulted, some of the prisoners said there had been severe beatings and perhaps a death. The prison authorities denied it, and that was that. There was never a word of follow-up to this story in any newspaper and one never heard it mentioned in private conversations. It was just simply not interesting. The public was never told what these men were in jail for, what their names were, or even if they had names. And yet it is more than possible that half of them, or two-thirds, or even all of them, were being held in preventive detention. Now, these conditions are no worse than in some other places and countries, including the state of Arkansas. But unless a middle-class public can see its own image reflected in someone like Gabrielle Russier nobody cares. "People held in preventive detention commit suicide all the time," said Casamayor. "They are humble persons. We never hear of them." As for prison conditions, it seemed to be taken for granted that they *should* be bad. In 1969 a man who had served seven years for a crime it then turned out he had not committed was retried and released. The prison chaplain said, "At twenty-six, he looks like an old man now. He has lost sixteen of his teeth, [as a result of] the prison diet." Although this interview was broadcast at least twice, it did not appear to shock anybody. A foreigner suggesting that there might be something wrong with the prison diet would be told—even by liberals—that jails are not supposed to be health resorts. On this subject, the deputy public prosecutor had the last word: "Where would we be if we gave up [performing our duties] on the pretext of deplorable penitentiary conditions or the psychological state of every person accused?"

. . .

Gabrielle's lawyers had made two demands for "provisional liberty," which were turned down, giving the impression that either the prisoner was dangerous or the charge very serious indeed. No one knows to this day why they were refused. The minister of justice said later that the question of her parole was "delicate" and that when she had been released after her first arrest the examining magistrate had received letters of protest from parents. It was taken for granted by the public now that her imprisonment was a form of pressure on Christian. She was not freed, in fact, until the day he gave himself up. He told someone that he had not realized she was still in jail, and perhaps that is true, though the papers were full of it. Once again he was packed off to stay with a relation somewhere else in France, and his parents, at their wits' end, even suggested that he join the navy. As far as Gabrielle was concerned, he seems to have vanished off the map. He was now eighteen. He had never been on his own, except as a runaway, and had never earned his living or been responsible for anyone else. He may have been unable to realize what it means exactly to have a prison record, to be in jail, to be parted from your children, to fall hopelessly into debt, to lose your job, and to be barred from your profession. He has said that he occasionally wrote to Gabrielle, but that she never answered. She seldom mentioned him in letters. It was her ex-husband, Michel Nogues, who had been loyal to her throughout, who met her as she came out of the prison gates. He was shocked at the change in her. Everyone who saw her in the three weeks between her release and her trial spoke of her altered manner. She trembled, she shrank away as if afraid of a blow, she could barely speak above a whisper—much of the symptoms of her nervous breakdown some eight or nine months before. She cried almost continually and seemed afraid of scoldings, like a child who has known too much harshness. Raymond Jean, who saw her at this time, wrote that she was "haggard, pale, undone, thin." She kept looking over her shoulder, as if she was afraid of being spied on, and she seemed to have trouble breathing. A woman friend who saw a great deal of her was convinced that this behavior was an act, and one of her lawyers thought so too. He said he believed she had "simulated" some of her symptoms, or at least exaggerated them, but that the "breakdown itself was real enough." Her entire conversation was about her life in prison and her terror and apprehension about the trial, which still loomed ahead. Christian was living somewhere with a relation. There was no contact between them. They seemed to have drifted out of each other's lives. A news magazine reproached him in an editorial for having abandoned her, but there was not much he could have done at this point except get in the way. She wore out her friends by repeating the same questions over and over: How strong were the Rossis? What would become of her children? Would she be barred from teaching? Was she the victim of a plot involving the Rossis, the law, and the Ministry of National Education? She felt she had been "crushed by a rock" and that she had wandered into a Kafka world. Between the time of her release from jail in June and her trial in July she was unable to cook, shop, look after her son Joël (her daughter was still in the holiday camp), or cope with even the simplest domestic situations. The writer Michel del Castillo has given an account of how a neighbor came into her darkened apartment one night and found Joël alone in his room and supperless, while Gabrielle cowered in an armchair in the living room. The neighbor asked her if the little boy had been given anything at all to eat. (It must be remembered that her children were not allowed to help themselves.) Gabrielle seemed unable to grasp the question or even understand what was being said to her. The kitchen was completely empty of food, as if she had not done any shopping for days.

"Timidly, Joël said, 'There are cornflakes in the cupboard.'

"As though seized by a sudden fit of madness, Gabrielle leaped from her chair and screamed, 'Cornflakes! Cornflakes! I've had enough about cornflakes! I never want to hear about cornflakes! Never again!' "

She then crept behind the refrigerator and crouched on the floor, sobbing. When the neighbor, who had gone back to her own apartment to prepare a meal for the child, returned half an hour later, she found Gabrielle in the same place, still crying. She told the neighbor, "They broke me in prison. There are times when I can't stand my own son anymore. Yesterday I kicked the cat. I'm finished."

Her symptoms may have been "simulated" but her worries were real. She had been suggested for the post of university lecturer at Aix-en-Provence, something for which she was amply qualified. Twenty professors met to vote on the appointment, among them Christian's father and Raymond Jean. Although Jean argued in her favor, she was turned down by a vote of eleven to nine. Then, two days before her trial, she received a letter asking her to repay the Ministry of National Education two months of her salary for the time she had been in prison. It seems harsh and bureaucratic, as if the Ministry of National Education had somehow been wondering where she was all that time. Of course, there is another side to it: during the academic year of 1968–9 she had hardly set foot in a classroom, for she had been given a long sick leave, and after her first arrest had been suspended with pay for several months. (The suspension was not punitive; the principal of the lyceé was afraid her presence might be "disruptive.") Gabrielle Russier did not pay back the two months' salary because she probably didn't have it. As the state's claim has never been revoked, this debt has been inherited by her twins. Joël and Valérie owe the Ministry of National Education two months of their late mother's salary, to be paid out of whatever their inheritance amounts to. Shortly before the trial, Gabrielle made an attempt to kill herself by taking barbiturates. She was found in time by a neighbor who persuaded her to see a psychiatrist. The psychiatrist said there was not much he could do, and he gave her a prescription for more sleeping pills.

In spite of her distraught state of mind, she did not lose her bearings. She pulled herself together enough to write to a mutual friend asking the friend to see if Christian might not be persuaded to appear in court at her trial on July 10. She thought that if the magistrates could see the tall bearded figure described in the accusation as "a child" it might take some of the opprobrium from the charge. However, he was not called, he did not testify, he made no deposition, and his presence was not considered "useful." Perhaps the testimony of a male minor is not taken into account (though a girl's might have been). What could he have said or written? He might have told a few truths —that when she wanted to end the affair he broke down her door; that he had instigated the trip to Italy; that he had begged her to fetch him in Germany; that he had threatened to run away from boarding school unless she came to see him (and then ran away anyway); and finally, of most capital importance, whether she was the first woman in his life or whether he'd had previous experiences and knew exactly what he was doing. Perhaps the court would have refused his deposition; on the other hand, it might have helped. In the *Nouvel-Observateur* interview in 1971, he says that Gabrielle was by no means his first lover. "I had already had other adventures [affairs] and as a general rule with women older than myself." But, he specifies, always with women who looked "relatively young."

A French trial of this sort is a three-cornered affair. There is the accused, Gabrielle, represented by her counsel; the *partie civile*, or plaintiffs—Christian's family, with *their* counsel; there is the public prosecutor, or his deputy, who represents something called the Public Ministry, which means society, the people of France. *Partie civile* is not really "plaintiff" as we use the term, but since the *partie civile* does not exist in Anglo-Saxon law there is no exact equivalent. Once the Rossis had lodged their complaint against "X" the matter was out of their hands and became entirely the affair of the Public Ministry. The public prosecutor and his deputies are not ordinary lawyers, but high-ranking magistrates. As their titles suggest, they conduct the prosecution, they ask for the sentence they think necessary, and if the jury or the presiding judge does not give the verdict or the sentence they ask for, they have the right to appeal. The lawyers representing the *partie civile* also question the witnesses and the defendant, so that it seems like two against one. What the plaintiffs—in this case the Rossis—are asking for, as a rule, are damages. The damages can be a large sum, or the symbolic one franc, the award of which confirms that the plaintiffs have been harmed morally, or mentally, or in their public stature. One of Gabrielle Russier's lawyers remarked drily—of the Rossis—"One would have expected more nonchalance [from Communists] for bourgeois principles, bourgeois morality, and the bourgeois police." At the Russier trial, the deputy public prosecutor had specific instructions from the *parquet* to ask for a thirteen-month suspended sentence. It was of enormous importance, for Georges Pompidou had just become president of the Republic, and the tradition is that a new president declares an amnesty for all sentences of less than twelve months. (All traffic fines still pending are wiped out.) If Gabrielle Russier were to receive a sentence of twelve months or less, she would come under the shelter of this amnesty; she would not have a police record, and there would be no legitimate reason to prevent her from teaching. That was why the prosecutor had received instructions to ask for thirteen months.

On the day of the trial the Palace of Justice was swarming with photographers and reporters. Gabrielle saw the father of Christian and had a curious exchange with him: as though afraid of being scolded, she told him it was not she who had invited the press. He reassured her. The concierge of the building watched her go by and said the equivalent of "dirty bitch" between her teeth. As often happens at a hearing in which a minor is involved, the court was cleared: some of the public who did not know this was customary were left with the impression that the details of her liaison were too filthy and scabrous for delicate ears. When the sentence was announced the next day, Gabrielle was not in court. (Her lawyers had obtained special permission for her to remain at home that day because of the usual cluster of neighborhood Eumenides.) She learned that she had been fined the equivalent of one hundred dollars and given a suspended sentence of twelve months, which came under the presidential amnesty. Her police record, as the French expression quaintly has it, "remained virginal." She shot off telegrams in all directions signed "Antigone" and "Phaedra," including one to her lawyer (signed "Antigone") that said, "Thank you. Long live the sun."

About thirty minutes after the sentence had been passed, the deputy prosecutor came up to Gabrielle's counsel in the Palace of Justice and said, "I am going to appeal *a minima.* I have just received instructions."

The full Latin phrase would have been *a minima paena,* meaning "the smallest sentence." This is the appeal that the Public Ministry (in the name of society) interjects when the ministry thinks that a sentence has been too light. It is very rare. One of Gabrielle's lawyers said that he knew of only ten such appeals between 1932 and 1969, and then in cases involving much more serious matters than the deviation of a seventeen-year-old boy by a woman. On the other hand, perhaps any aspect of public morality is a serious matter in France: In the summer of 1970 there was an appeal by the Public Ministry against the decision of a lower court acquitting a Bordeaux publisher on a charge of distributing pornography. What he had distributed were films intended for health and nudist clubs. The court of appeal also acquitted him, because the films were innocent. It was a decision that created a precedent: until 1970 the courts had been extremely severe where "reproductions of the human body in its entirety" were concerned. This is merely to point out that Public Ministry appeals may be rare, but they are certainly selective. As a rule, if a defendant accepts the verdict of the court the matter ends there. But if he has the impertinence to appeal for a smaller sentence or a lower fine the office of the public prosecutor will lodge a counter appeal *a minima*, which may make the defendant wish he had accepted what he was given in the first place. "A sort of dreadful game," is what Maître Naud has called this. What was absolutely without precedence was the speed with which the Public Ministry issued its orders—within half an hour after a sentence.

"In my career of thirty-seven years at the bar, I have never seen an appeal so rapid," said Maître Naud.

None of this was taking place in secret, but well lighted

by the radio and the press, and accompanied by a volume
of comment, debate, and protest almost unparalleled in
recent French life. Victor Hugo's celebrated remark, "The
law is a machine that cannot move without crushing
someone," was quoted by everyone who could remember
it. There was scarcely any area of public life where
Gabrielle Russier's name was not mentioned. What
seemed to outrage public opinion now was the dispro-
portion between her offense and the weight of her punishment, and to an onlooker who knew little about the
penal code the courts did seem capricious when it came
to sentencing. Thirteen months, or even twelve months,
seemed severe compared with decisions handed down on
charges that were much graver. A woman shot her husband to death because he was politically ambitious, did
not want her to meet his friends, had a mistress, and had
threatened to leave her. She was acquitted and as she left
the court the omnipresent knot of neighborhood female
furies cried, "Bravo, Yvonne." In 1969 a man in a suburb
of Paris stabbed a neighbor to death because the neighbor's
little girl had been bouncing a ball against his door. First
he kicked the child, then he called up the stairs to the
child's father, "Come down if you are a man," then he
got a knife and ran it into him. He was given a suspended
sentence. In 1970 two grown men, brothers, got in an
argument over what to feed their dog. One killed the
other. The sentence was two years. Children are regularly
abused and ill-treated and some of them die of their
wounds. What are the sentences? Suspended . . . two
years . . . eighteen months. Nothing is as irritating to
lawyers as comparisons of this kind, for in a French

murder trial the jury is not asked if the defendant *did
it*, but if he is *guilty*. (It is absolutely untrue that an
accused person is considered guilty until proved innocent
in France; it only seems that way. There is no such thing as
a plea of "not guilty" in French law. The accused can only
protest his innocence and attempt to prove that he should
not have been arrested—that the state has no case. The jury
is not asked if the prisoner committed a crime, but if he is
guilty of the charge the state has made against him.
Example: "She is guilty of cold-blooded murder." "No! No!
I loved him! I wept as I pulled the trigger!" Not guilty.) As
the Russier case was heard *in camera,* no one can know
what was said, or what was held against her. Her sentence
showed only that it must be tricky to be a defendant when
some ministry or other has decided to make an example of
you. In the case of the man who stabbed his neighbor, the
court expressed sympathy for persons who live in noisy
and jerry-built apartment houses. In the case of dead or
battered children the poverty or the alcoholism or the
idiocy of the mother are taken into account. Gabrielle
Russier had no such elements in her favor.

The Public Ministry now began to suggest that the
appeal was nothing but routine. This gave the impression that the law was a great tidal wave no one knew
how to stop. But there were respected lawyers who came
forward to say, in public, that the appeal *a minima* was
not routine, and that the law was being used as a repressive instrument. In times of stress and confusion the
public in France relies for information on those radio
stations that are not government-owned, Europe 1,
Radio-Television Luxembourg, and, in the south, Radio

Monte Carlo. Just how "independent" commercial stations are is another matter, but at least they seem to be free of a certain kind of unimaginative censorship. It was over these "peripheral stations," as they are called, that the ordinary public, the more than fifty percent of the population who never read newspapers, now learned what *a minima* was about, and that the appeal was not routine, and that the law was something mysterious called *"du Kafka."* But Casamayor was also heard, and he said that the law was not a Kafka mystery, nor was justice inevitably unjust: "The whole thing was an operation and she was its object." She was not the victim of something dark and compelling, but merely of "men with opinions." Who were these men? They were in the Ministry of National Education, said some of her colleagues. Maître Naud, who was preparing to defend her before the court of appeal at Aix-en-Provence, had every intention of bringing up the rumor that the Ministry of National Education had asked the Public Ministry to make absolutely certain she could never teach again. There were people who found this idea hard to swallow, at the time. The Ministry of National Education has an enormous budget, an army of persons to deal with, it is responsible for everything from kindergartens to universities, and it seemed unlikely that men at the very top level of public life had nothing better to do than pursue and persecute a woman because she had once hidden a runaway. In time it began to seem that if she *was* being hounded, it must be for something left out of the penal code—for having had a young lover. The difference in age between Gabrielle and Christian was fifteen years, but she was often talked about as "old enough to have been his mother." Her opponents (and she had them) described her as an aging nymphomaniac in search of her lost youth. This insistence on her age sounded curious in a country where women are considered young much longer than in the English-speaking world. Press accounts of any news event will describe as "a young woman" virtually any woman under fifty, and the young boy infatuated with an older or married woman is a favorite subject in novels: *Chéri, Le diable au corps, Le rouge et le noir, Le blé en herbe* come to mind one after the other. Some of Gabrielle Russier's friends thought that she was harassed for having sided with her students during the riots of 1968 and that her trial was really political. But in that case, why Gabrielle Russier? Professor Rossi had been an active militant, he was a Communist, and not only was he not being harassed, but he was receiving the active assistance of the law. The "men with opinions" Casamayor had spoken of perhaps had opinions about her morals and nothing else. Later, the deputy public prosecutor removed any ambiguity by putting it in the plainest possible language: "An inscription on her police record was needed so as to facilitate disciplinary action and remove her from her post. She deserved it."

It stands to reason that a section of the public thought she deserved it too, for the office of the public prosecutor rests on more than the "ideas" of a few men. There were the parents who had objected when she was freed after her first arrest, for instance. She had women against her, mothers of sons, or just women anxious to let the world know they would never have fallen in love with a minor

whatever the circumstances. Letters condemning her continued to arrive at women's magazines long after her
death. Reams of similar letters were read aloud over
Radio Monte Carlo (passion over this case reached an
extraordinary pitch in the south) and Gabrielle Russier
finally became a subject better not brought up at dinner
parties, like the Dreyfus affair several generations before.
One other count against her was the fact that she was
divorced. It sounds improbable in a country where divorce is accepted, relatively easy to obtain, and widely
practiced. But there exists a prejudice against a divorced
woman not just in France but nearly everywhere. It comes
to the surface if a private situation becomes a moral
issue: then the person involved is not just a woman, but
a divorcée . . . though in similar circumstances no one is
ever likely to pull a face over a divorced man. Even in
the United States, the last place one might expect it, this
mental prohibition exists. "He liked the company of 35-
year-old blonde divorcées" turned up in *Time* in 1970,
and what it meant was "he liked the company of sleazy
women." Take out the words "blonde divorcées" and
substitute "unmarried women" and see how the sentence
sounds. So that if "divorcée" is journalists' shorthand for
"floozie" even in America, what can it be in a country as
Catholic and conservative as France? "A divorced woman
with two children" clanged away like a clock endlessly
striking, though her divorce had been the least scandalous
imaginable: she and Michel Nogues had discovered they
did not want the same kind of life, and they parted
amicably. He remained her friend, and stood by her
through the trial and after. Each time her civil status

("divorced") was mentioned in a certain tone of voice one wondered if things had changed all that much since a French book of etiquette advised, "The divorced woman removes her wedding ring, she resumes her maiden name, and she tries to live a discreet and retired life." Part of the public also believed that she should be made an example, otherwise there would be nothing to stop adolescents from leaving home, disobeying, and starting up love affairs with elderly persons. Probably no ministry of education anywhere would want its instructors to keep falling in love with the children they teach. But perhaps not very many would. The French humorist Pierre Daninos has pointed out that whenever one does anything even slightly out of the way in France, the response is invariably, "But what if *everyone* did that?" There must be millions of students who would not sleep with their professors even if it were legal. Other arguments were more serious—she was a teacher, entrusted with the care of young persons outside their own homes. Replacing Christian's parents, she had betrayed the trust they—and all the other parents—had placed in her. Also, as a teacher she was a civil servant and bound by a code demanding respectable behavior. "Gabrielle Russier gave a bad example," said the deputy public prosecutor, "because she scoffed at parental authority. If she had at least made due apology . . ." It would require a volume the size of a telephone book to record the positions taken and abandoned, the opinions asked for and supplied, the long debates in the form of letters, the speeches, the declarations, the statements of belief. Tracts littered the pavements around universities and lycées, and posters

were gummed up in Aix-en-Provence and Marseilles accusing society, the Fifth Republic, the teaching system,
bourgeois hypocrisy, and Christian's family. Libelous
gossip circulated wildly—everyone knew someone who
knew that the Rossis had tried to have their son certified
insane (they had not) or that they had all sorts of dubious
reasons for wanting to break Gabrielle Russier for life.
The Rossis had not asked for the appeal *a minima:* once
they had Christian at home that was all they wanted. It
became impossible to point this out because hardly anyone would listen. The voices of officialdom went on saying
that the appeal was only a legal routine, and lawyers in
private practice continued to retort that it was not. "They
always ask for the maximum sentence and we nearly
always get less," said one lawyer. "If the prosecutor were
to appeal *a minima* each time, it would never end. Every
case would go to appeal." When this particular appeal was
no longer necessary because the defendant had killed herself, it was the turn of the minister of justice to explain,
also through a radio station, "It was all legal. Everything
was done within the law."

"They have made a mountain out of nothing," Gabrielle
wrote despairingly from jail, and that was how it began
to seem: for what, exactly, had she done? Unless one
accepted a love affair as something criminal, it seemed
absurd to refer the case to a court of appeal. She had
fallen in love and lost her head; encouraging Christian to
lie to his parents was perhaps a fault, a failure as their
friend, but at that point she was neither friend nor
teacher: if every weakness and subterfuge for which in-
fatuation is responsible were punishable by law no prison

in the world would be large enough. As an adult involved with a minor, did she introduce him to some advanced form of vice? Did she make him drink? Give him drugs? Unlikely. She was, if anything, slightly puritanical. Did she make him unhappy, torture him, sequester him, spy on him, and make his life hell? Did she prevent him from studying? One letter she wrote him must certainly be the least erotic message any woman ever sent her lover. It was an outline of work: Christian was to study Italian, he was to see two movies a week (one "cultural" and one anything), he was to read one French novel a week and a few chapters of a foreign novel . . . As her ex-husband said, she was a born educator. "The contact between them was not null," said a lawyer. "In fact, it was profitable." He must have meant for Christian: by that time Gabrielle was dead.

The shock of good news immediately followed by bad would have unsettled a character much tougher than Gabrielle Russier's. Her fears and worries about the new trial became so obsessive that a doctor advised a sleep cure, which she undertook in a hospital. From there she went to a rest home in the Pyrenees "to avoid the depression that follows a sleep cure." Once again she tried to kill herself and once again was found in time. Her letters spoke of her terrors: her lack of money, rent owing on her apartment, the fear that her children might become charges of the state. When she wrote, "I am not dramatizing. It is the situation that is dramatic," she was speaking the truth. Even an unimaginative woman would have felt helpless and beset. She had virtually no one in the world. Her parents were elderly and her mother a helpless invalid. Her ex-husband had done what he could, but he was not wealthy, and he was, after all, a man she had divorced. She had friends, but they were neither rich nor powerful, and she herself, as the product of a hard middle-class society where the expression "everyone has his own problems" strikes the ear rather frequently, probably did not expect much. She did ask, in one letter, if a public subscription might not be opened in the left-wing weekly *Nouvel-Observateur*, which shows how desperate she must have been for help and money. The other people in the rest home had "only psychological problems, not real difficulties." But her defenses—like theirs, perhaps—were almost entirely eroded. She wrote "if something should happen to me" on August 1.

She left the rest home at the end of August and came back to a Marseilles that had been emptied by the last weekend of the summer holidays. It was a Saturday night. She was alone. No one met her at the station. The apartment house she lived in was as quiet as the rest of the city—nearly everyone had gone away. It seems incredible that the nurses and doctors and psychiatrists who had been dealing with her let her go off without getting in touch with some member of her family or a close friend. She did not bother to unpack. The next day—Sunday—some-one came to see her. She and the visitor had a drink and she made coffee—the cups and the glasses were found. After the unknown guest departed she sealed the cracks of the doors and windows with clothes and old newspapers, shut the electric meter to avoid the risk of an explosion, and turned on the gas. She lay down on the bed and swallowed all the sleeping pills she had in the house. Firemen broke down the door on Monday. They found Gabrielle in a blue dressing gown, and the empty glasses and cups. There was no inquest, no autopsy, and the police did not even examine the glasses for fingerprints. Her visitor has never come forward to say what their last conversation was about.

The lawyer who was to have represented her at the court of appeal received two messages in one day: one was the news that his client was dead, and the other a letter from her ex-husband, written a few days earlier. Michel Nogues was disturbed at the idea of a new trial and over the sort of publicity his ex-wife had been subjected to. He wanted the public to see "her real face," and he spoke of "her high moral worth." Their marriage had failed because of their opposing characters and points of view. Nevertheless, "I consider my ex-wife morally impeccable." She was also "an exceptional mother" and "an educator by vocation." She had been raised in a tradition of service; she "likes to serve, using 'serve' in its most noble meaning, the Anglo-Saxon sense of the word." This must have been the letter she had asked him to write, and which she mentioned two days before she killed herself, remarking that her father had said it would be "useful." Long after her death, in March 1971, Michel Nogues wrote another letter in Gabrielle's defense, this time in response to the *Paris-Match* interview with Professor Rossi. He ends his long letter to *Paris-Match* with: "Gabrielle [was] courageous, in love with the absolute, incapable of dissimulating or lying, determined to stand up to the forces raised against her which encircled her and finally crushed her."

A few days later Madame Rossi agreed to be interviewed together with Christian. The outcry against her family was so enormous that she may have wanted to state her side of it. A reporter from Radio-Television Luxembourg was allowed in the house with his recording equipment. Her voice was educated, hard, slightly masculine, and—not surprisingly—slightly emotional. Christian mumbled, and suddenly his mother's voice covered his: "Stop! Stop!" "Christian clenches his fists, stops talking, leaves the room," said the reporter. The next day he was interviewed by the same person, but without his mother, in a café. "I can't speak, I can't speak," he began saying. Then, responding to questions, he said that yes, he had been shut up in a psychiatric clinic. "It was traumatic." Why had this been done? "Well—you know—parents are responsible for their children. They have every right." Was it true that he had also been sent to an observation center? Why? "Because I was considered a delinquent minor. By my parents—I think." It had been "their decision." Had he loved Gabrielle? (What a question! Was he likely to say no a few days after her suicide?) "Yes." Had she loved him? "I think so," said Christian, making a careful division of responsibility; for who can say what the other person really thinks and feels? Did he feel to blame for her death? Absolutely not. "Justice" was responsible, he said. "And certainly my parents. I think so. I can't reproach them too much, not for the moment." But then he decided he blamed more than merely "justice" and his parents: there was the appeal *a minima*, and also her sleep cure, "if it is true that she took one," his uncertainty showing that they had not been in touch before the end, that he had had no idea what was happening to her or where she was. You weren't suicidal after *your* sleep cure? the reporter asked. "No, because I love life." Also, he was sure he would stay alive: "At least, I hope so!" He laughed, as if he and the interviewer were conspirators—at any rate, both living. He sounded charming and young. "She loved life too," he said quickly, overtaking any impression of carelessness. "But she was desperate. I know people who committed suicide after taking the sleep cure." One wondered what he meant, exactly. How many of his friends had killed themselves? How many had been obliged to undergo such extreme therapy? If it was true that this treatment was such a frequent cause of suicide that an eighteen-year-old had known several cases, wouldn't the law have stepped in, or a medical association? "Every day she saw that the day when we might perhaps live together was further and further away," he said, without explaining that, either, for every day brought him nearer his majority and freedom to choose. Apart from their brief and confused love affair when he was seventeen, they had not been together much. One wondered if they had really known each other well. Did Christian accuse anyone *in particular?* "I accuse everything," he said suddenly. "Society. Everything. Society, and judges, and parents. I accuse all reactionary and bourgeois parents." It sounded like a lesson, like memory work. It was not the voice of the person who had laughed a minute earlier and said, "I love life." He sounded like a parrot with a Marseilles accent. "My future is my own business," he went on, in a new voice, a normal voice. "I won't forget what happened, but I wish everybody else would." Two weeks later he vanished again. He had not run away. "He is exiled," said someone on the radio who knew the family. The subject of Gabrielle Russier was taboo in the Rossi household, because of the two younger children. He was described as "torn" between his loyalty to his family and his rejection of them. By the spring of 1970, he was living in Paris and was said to have broken with his parents. He was nineteen. His "correspondent," the person appointed to keep an eye on a minor, was the Protestant minister who had married Gabrielle and Michel Nogues and had christened her twins. In June, Christian sat for his baccalaureate examinations in his and Gabrielle Russier's old school, then he came back to Paris "to find employment." His clergyman correspondent said that Christian was in a bad way. "Although I am a Christian, I would have found it hard to forgive my parents had I been in his place," said the minister. He was not referring to Gabrielle, but to Christian's having been committed to the care of a juvenile court and to the sleep cure. "He must be left alone, in peace. Anything could happen now. His greatest terror is of being sent back to a psychiatric clinic. He is obsessed with this fear." Christian evidently failed the examinations he sat for in Marseilles, because in the spring of 1971 he was still studying "by correspondence." The film of the story

"*Mourir d'Aimer*" had brought him into prominence, and he was widely photographed, heard on the radio, and interviewed both directly and indirectly. He was supposed to be working as an assistant projectionist in a cinema in the Latin Quarter at about $260 a month (*France-Soir*, January 13, 1971), though for some reason he told an interviewer, "I work. Don't ask me where or at what, I work and earn my living." He is now very hard on his parents in interviews. When he was asked over Radio-Luxembourg if he thought he would ever see his family again, he answered that sometimes one can't help meeting people by accident. In the *Nouvel-Observateur* interview he says he does not love his parents and never did.

Gabrielle died on September 1, 1969. Professor Rossi (according to his version) persuaded Christian to go and stay with friends in Paris, to get him away from publicity and the press in Marseilles. On the fifth of September, four days after her death, Christian sent his family a postcard: "Paris, 5 September 1969. Dear Everyone, I am writing to tell you that I arrived in Paris with some delay [he means the train was late]. Monday night I went to see *Hair*. Finish your séjour [holiday] without worrying. A bientôt. Kisses. Christian."

Not long after Gabrielle's death, President Pompidou held a televised press conference. The last question, a totally unexpected one, was asked by a reporter from Radio Monte Carlo: what had the president done about the Russier case, and, in view of the outcome, what did he think? "I won't tell you what I did," said the president, "but this is what I think." To those watching, he seemed truly taken aback, as if the question were the last one in the world he expected in a conference devoted to the Common Market and planes for Israel. He hesitated, as though he were deeply moved and trying to control his feelings, and at the same time wanted to be certain that what he would say would be the right thing. President Pompidou is an *agrégé* in French literature (as Gabrielle Russier had been) and the editor of an anthology of French poetry. Now he recited the first verse of a poem by Paul Eluard, as though drawing it out of the very back of his memory. This is a poem "about" something, as a story is: about a girl whose hair was cut off after the Liberation, probably because she had slept with Germans, and who was punished to divert attention from real collaborators, the truly guilty. The poet—and the president, apparently—felt "remorse" only for the victim who lay on the pavement "with the look of a lost child," who resembled "the dead" who have perished "because they were loved." When poetry is translated, the result is either not faithful, not poetry, or not English. This is the verse that President Pompidou repeated:

> *Comprenne qui voudra*
> *Moi mon remords ce fut*
> *La malheureuse qui resta*
> *Sur le pavé*
> *La victime raisonnable*
> *A la robe déchirée*
> *Au regard d'enfant perdue*

> *Découronée défigurée*
> *Celle qui ressemble aux morts*
> *Qui sont morts pour être aimés.*

No one knew what the president had meant by "what I did," for he could not have interfered with legal procedure. The minister of justice had already explained that the magistrates of the Public Ministry were not obliged to consult anyone, and had acted within the law and "according to conscience." What everyone seized on now were phrases from the Eluard poem: "my remorse," "the reasonable" (i.e., well behaved) "victim," and, above all, "dead for having been loved." To a foreigner it seemed an extraordinary moment for television—a great public figure caught off guard, and the head of a highly literate nation turning to literature in order to explain himself. The effect was somewhat lessened when the reporter from Radio Monte Carlo said that the question had been planted, and that he had been "approached" and told that if he mentioned the Russier trial no one would object. If true, it is interesting that an independent peripheral station was used, and not one of the government's own channels. The president of the Republic can't be responsible for every "approach" made in his name. His slight hesitation before replying, his emotion, and his surprise seemed too spontaneous to have been counterfeit. Perhaps he had already wondered what he would say if the question should be asked. Anyway, someone asked it.

.   .   .

Before her death Gabrielle Russier wrote, "If only what is happening to me could at least serve for something!" One thing did happen—a law was voted making preventive detention the exception rather than the rule. Some lawyers were still skeptical: they pointed out that under the penal code as it existed it was already supposed to be the exception. The minister of justice declared that the new law had nothing whatever to do with Gabrielle Russier, while the brother of a student arrested during a university riot wrote to *Le Monde* in July 1970 protesting that his brother had been in jail since April and that the examining magistrate had now taken off for a month's vacation in Turkey.

For the rest: two chalk inscriptions remained for a long time on the door of her apartment—"Z," meaning "he lives," and "Immortal Gatito." Her students had put them there.

Professor Rossi declared, "If it were all to be done again, I would do the same thing."

The president of the most important parent-student association in France said, "This boy was lucky to have met someone like Gabrielle Russier."

The Rossis brought a lawsuit against the author of a book about the case and were awarded damages. Although Christian had given much of the information and had read the proofs, he was still a minor (nineteen) and could be named as a plaintiff whether he wanted to be or not. Some of the damages were asked in his name.

A film was whisked into production, to be called *To Die for Love*, a reference to the Eluard poem. François Truffaut broadcast an appeal to Annie Girardot, asking her not to take the role of Gabrielle, "who hated gossip and had died of it," and accusing the director of the movie of "robbing the pockets of the dead." His appeal was unheeded and stills were soon issued of Annie Girardot with her hair cut and darkened and looking rather like Gabrielle. The director retorted that the film did not take place in Marseilles, but up north in Rouen, and that it was not about a lycée, but a book shop. One day a woman of thirty meets a tall, bearded, seventeen-year-old Maoist whose parents . . . Moreover, said the director, Christian knew about the movie and approved.

A new *affaire* held the attention of the entire nation: A man had shut himself up in his house with his two children, saying he would kill them and himself if the police stormed the house. The police stormed the house, and he killed his two children and himself. Administrative bungling seemed to be the rule; *l'affaire de Cestas* and *l'affaire Russier* were mentioned together and always with the same question: who is to blame for all this? The answer was, it was legal, everyone was doing his duty, and we are probably all to blame. The deputy public prosecutor of the Russier case summed it up for everyone: "I, as a public minister, did nothing more than my job . . . From that point of view, we are all responsible, we are all assassins."

This was a useful last word, for when everyone is responsible then nobody is, and that is comfortable, finally.

For Gabrielle

Publishing letters from someone who has died is a delicate matter. I am doing so—aware of the legitimate hesitations of Gabrielle Russier's family and closest friends, but with their consent—for two reasons. First, after everything that has been written about Gabrielle by those who knew her and those who did not (and I do not expect special treatment for my own words), I felt it was important to let her express herself, to give her "the word." Second, I felt it would be wrong not to bring to light these letters, which, to my mind, constitute a human document of exceptional quality. By their very nature they allow everyone to witness what could be called Gabrielle's "rehabilitation." Her troubles are reflected here with devastating truth. Step by step we follow the progress of her despair, and sometimes her hope. These letters explain what she lived through better than all the articles that have been written about her, and they ring true. As I have said, they are authentically "the diary of a torment." At a time when we pay particular attention to personal revelation in literature, the letters often seem like the work of a true writer.

Most of them were written from prison, during the

second stay in Les Baumettes in April, May, and June 1969. A number, however, are dated earlier and serve as points of reference. Finally, others, rarer but particularly important, were sent from La Recouvrance, the convalescent home in the Pyrenees, a few weeks, and sometimes a few days, before Gabrielle's suicide.

My deepest thanks must be addressed to the correspondents who were kind enough to authorize the publication of these letters.

I saw Gabrielle Russier for the first time in 1962. I say "saw" intentionally. She was sitting slightly to the right in the first row of a small lecture hall—the Blondel Amphitheater—in the old faculty of letters at Aix. (Today, by closing my eyes, I can recall the scene with extraordinary precision.) She was then twenty-four. After several periods overseas, I had just been appointed to the faculty, and I had undertaken to give a course on Eluard. As I spoke I gazed at the audience; my glance was arrested fairly swiftly by this young woman with very short hair, a strange triangular-shaped face, a sharp profile, and something a little unusual and off-putting in her expression which made me think vaguely of either a cat or a sheep. One day I had suggested that during the next session the students listen to some of Eluard's poems recited by Gérard Philipe and by Eluard himself. Since it was difficult to get hold of the faculty's only phonograph, I had asked if there was anyone in the audience who could lend his own equipment. At the end of the lecture Gabrielle had come forward to say that if I wanted she would bring a phonograph. On the appointed day she came not only with her little carrying case, but with another recording by the poet, different from my own. In the days that followed I had several conversations with Gabrielle. I took an interest in her work, and she often came to speak to me at the end of my class. During one of these conversations we discovered we had both lived in Morocco in the past and had both been implicated in a business that had caused a certain scandal at the time—the so-called 481 Affair. Four hundred and eighty-one Frenchmen from Morocco had signed and made public a manifesto demanding the opening of negotiations between the French government and the provisional government of the Algerian republic, based on the recognition of Algeria's independence. This happened well before the Manifesto of the 121, at a time when war was stirring up the whole of North Africa, and when the idea of an independent Algeria had not made much headway in the public mind. Therefore this stand was very badly received in certain quarters, notably the French Embassy and among the traditional French colonialists. All manner of counter-measures and reprisals followed, and in particular various punitive measures were officially taken against the most noteworthy signers. Like most of the teachers involved in this affair, Gabrielle, who at the time was teaching at the Moulay Abdullah College in Casablanca, had some problems, but the establishment where she worked was under Moroccan jurisdiction and her difficulties could not go too far. Mine, on the other hand, knew no bounds, because at this point I lost my position and found myself "recalled" to France between one day and the next under the most brutal conditions. In any case, and this is what is important, when Gabrielle reminded me of these events I had a curious retrospective feeling of solidarity with her. The affair had left a considerable mark on me and had had multiple consequences on my life. The thought that Gabrielle had experienced the same shocks, breathed the same atmosphere of "sound and fury," made me feel strangely close and brotherly toward her. I immediately recognized her as a leftist who had known how to face up to her responsibilities under circumstances which were not particularly conducive to this line of behavior; certain names she mentioned made it apparent to me that she had had friends among the very drafters of the appeal and among the most committed founders of the movement. All of a sudden I no longer saw her as a student but as a colleague. She was very young to have taught at the Moulay Abdullah College, which had a reputation for being a "tough" establishment where the work was by no means restful. I found it difficult to imagine her with her slight frame and sharp little gaze opposing those big Moroccan kids who filled the senior classes. She explained to me that when her husband, an engineer, was stationed in Casablanca, she knew that the schools were short of instructors and had no trouble in obtaining this post, despite her then relatively modest level of academic achievement.

I recall these facts because they are precise, but in the coming year nothing of note followed these first meetings. Gabrielle was, without doubt, an excellent student (I remember a very good paper she did on Verlaine), but a student who little by little rejoined the others, blended in with them. She accomplished the work that was expected of her, passed her examinations, finished the year. Then she dealt with other professors, temporarily left the faculty, and disappeared—in any case for me.

Perhaps I should begin here to say who Gabrielle Russier was (known during her lifetime by her married name, Gabrielle Nogues, as if her maiden name—Russier—had, by some strange return-to-origins effect, been held in reserve to designate the other person she has become since her death). I shall pause a second to examine her background. She was French-American. To put it precisely she had a French father and an American mother. No particular conclusion may be drawn from that, unless the difference in her parents' sociocultural behavior could have been at the root of one of those curious "hereditary contradictions" which occasionally produce such surprising results. All the more so because this union appears to have taken place under the sign of romantic chance—a meeting at the Paris Opéra (Gabrielle's mother was very musical). She herself reminded me of this the other day in her apartment in an "alley" in the seventh arrondissement where she lives, a semi-recluse, almost an invalid, haunted now by all the painful images which tumble around in her head, all the bother from the journalists raging in her ears. She has remained very "American," voluble, with something that explains the hint of whimsy found in her daughter. She told me that her family was originally from Utah, the Mormon country, that Gabrielle's grandfather was called George Smith, and raised horses in Logan near Salt Lake City. All of a sudden, as I listened to her, I saw this rancher in the midst of his beasts in the vast plains of the desert state. My mind wandered. She never spoke about this. Her grandmother was of Farnes stock. The very old grandmother is still alive today in a little town in Idaho. It seems that Gabrielle wrote her regularly in English (for my part I never heard her say one word of English, but, obviously, she had command of this language, just as she had command of Spanish, which she used to sing very well). I shall end this American parenthesis here. I think that it can serve as a sort of indirect portrait. It is a difficult portrait; one which I consider it wise to "approach" obliquely, from an angle.

Next there was the "new novel." You may find it strange that I have selected the new novel as a sort of period, a *moment* in Gabrielle's life. Yet I don't think it is wrong. In 1964 her curiosity about the latest forms of current literature started to grow, and it was then that she came back to see me to ask a number of questions on contemporary novelistic forms. She devoted several chapters in her thesis to the "new novel" and in particular to works like *Portrait d'un inconnu* [Sarraute]; *Passage de Milan* and *La modification* [Butor]; *Les gommes* and *La jalousie* [Robbe-Grillet]; *Le vent, L'herbe,* and *La route des Flandres* [Claude Simon]. I have a copy of this paper in front of me, and in leafing through it I am struck by the extremely rigorous method which is apparent on every page; Gabrielle had based her research on stylistic studies, on works of statistical analysis which required a determination on her part not to advance any theory without either verification or proof and demonstrated that she could have become a brilliant linguist. It is curious, however, that every page of this paper, which is so scientific in appearance, full of charts and diagrams, bears witness to the most direct, the most immediate, the most intuitive understanding of the intimate substance of the fictional work. And the inscription at the beginning is not a linguistic reference but this quotation from Claude Simon: "This kind of substance, congealed and graying, which is time past." Today (for me at least) this suddenly has a singular and disturbing resonance.

I cannot forget Gabrielle as she was when she met Claude Simon—awkward and eaten up with curiosity at the same time, alternately shy and impulsive in her questions, attempting to better understand, to better *capture* the man who had written the texts she had spent so long examining, to read him like one of his own books. Later she had the same experience, although in a much more transitory manner, with other "new novelists" who came to Aix to address the students; it was the open season (how near and yet how far) when the new novel commanded vast university audiences. Thus she had the opportunity to meet Robbe-Grillet, Michel Butor, Jean Ricardou at some length—to eat with them, to question them and listen to them at leisure, to pursue her inquiry. But the meeting with Simon remained something special, difficult to forget, engraved upon her memory.

Then there was the summer of 1965. I was returning from a trip to Finland. I saw Gabrielle again.

I am stopping here in an attempt to sketch Gabrielle as she was at that time. It is not easy for several reasons. The most obvious is that so much without rhyme or reason has been written about her in the press, so much that is misleading, that it is difficult to dig into this pile of greater and lesser distortions to find the simple truth. Also, it is not easy to capture Gabrielle. I shall not return to the physical portrait I sketched at the beginning of this introduction. You can say whatever you want about someone's appearance, it depends on how you look at him. But you have to look. She was, in truth, neither ugly nor beautiful, but both at the same time and that in a very seductive and personal manner. Some days she seemed rumpled, on others radiant. But her small frame, short hair, pointed features, anxious eyes were constants, details which have contributed to the "Gatito" myth. Few photos among those that were published by the papers are happy or convincing. There is one—where she is seated in her car, her chin raised a little, the profile clean, the gaze steady, the expression serious and tense—which seems to me perhaps the most faithful.

As far as her character goes, things are more difficult to pin down. In Le Monde of September 13, 1969, I wrote that she had something of Gide's Alissa, of Antigone, and of an Antonioni heroine at one and the same time. I have no illusion about the significance of such remarks, written in the heat of the moment. Let us say that they can serve as points of reference. In recalling Alissa, I was alluding to Gabrielle's Protestant upbringing and to a certain interior unreasonableness

which could lead her to a strange kind of getting outside of herself. In referring to Antigone, I was stressing
everything that was stubborn, challenging, and occasionally exasperating about her. In speaking of one of
Antonioni's heroines, I was thinking of those solitary,
sighing women, wedded to both happiness and unhappiness, torn, absent, helpless, like Claudia in L'Avventura.
I don't know whether Gabrielle would have liked these
literary comparisons (I could have added others, Vio-
laine or Chloë, why not?). All those who were drawn
to follow her drama have had the impression that she
consciously embellished the circumstances of her life
with literary allusions, and it is true that her correspondence (as you will be able to judge) demonstrates a certain propensity for this type of reference. As for me, I
am merely attempting to "place" her in the eyes of
those who did not know her.

I have also written that she was possessed by "a
demon of destruction," a permanent temptation to
push matters to the limit, to the furthest extreme. A
statement which appeared to be ambiguous and which
people have used to justify the idea that she destroyed
whatever she touched, losing others at the same time
as herself, and that there was a sense of fatalism about
her. I would reply that in actual fact Gabrielle always
seemed to me to embody that form of destructive hyper-
lucidity which makes relationships with other people
difficult and occasionally impossible, that sometimes
this took on an exaggerated form, but I would add that
this nullifying tension was the measure of her refusal
to compromise; that is why I spoke of limits and ex-

tremes. This could account for an abrupt and aggressive streak in her, but also for the most unexpected tenderness and gaiety. In addition there were her intelligence —an essentially "organizational" one which could be observed in her university work as well as in the way she kept house and went about her daily life—her extreme tact, discretion, delicacy, care in all things, and above all her moral and physical energy, the ability to resist which astonished all those who witnessed it (even more astonishing in contrast with the physical exterior) and which right up until the end hid from even her closest friends what was so deeply vulnerable in her.

This is not the portrait of a saint. Gabrielle had faults too (like everyone, and occasionally more than everyone), and irritating character traits. I can imagine that there were those who must have been exasperated by certain qualities I was moved to "bestow" on her persistently in the statements I made over Radio Luxembourg or Radio Monte Carlo. "A remarkable young woman." "An exceptional young woman." This means nothing, as I know very well. She was not unusual. She knew what she wanted. She had a huge appetite for self-realization and for "grasping" other people's motivations. She employed these gifts very skillfully, occasionally overdoing it. She did not overlook the values of flirtation or flattery; she armed herself by disarming others. The result was that the atmosphere around her was often tense. Those close to her would testify to this, and probably this is the time to bring up certain matters about her family life. In the period I have just described, Gabrielle was in the process of getting a separation from her husband. She had said to me one day that she was moving, setting up home alone with her two children. I learned bit by bit that a conflict had arisen between her and her husband which had less to do with an outright misunderstanding than with basic incompatibility. They had both decided to go their own ways. Later (very much later) the divorce would take place. Here again it would be imprudent to make an argument for some kind of imbalance in Gabrielle on the basis of this episode. It is rare for separations to take place in such an undramatic way. Michel Nogues and his wife remained friends right up to the end, they saw each other regularly, and if their divorce was evidently not without effect on Gabrielle's destiny, in the final analysis it merely testifies to her loneliness.

She had two children, twins, Joël and Valérie, who, at that time, must have been six. She raised them with unwavering confidence and care; but there was something strange in the way the children often remained quietly in their rooms removed from the center of activity, as if participation in the community, meeting the world of adults, was fraught with danger.

Gabrielle sensed this, was frightened for them and for herself. To her eyes, Joël was in full bloom. Valérie was more secretive, less well adapted, a prey to her scholastic difficulties, already projecting the image of a "woman" who was to be considered with anxiety.

I have attempted this sketch to say as simply as possible (and I repeat) who Gabrielle was. Or rather what she was not—neurotic, unstable, hysterical, the "captious" woman that people have often gone to some length to see in her. *I do not deny that she did have a troubling capacity for giving vent to a certain type of negativism (especially—and I shall return to this point —in her social life) and even for multiplying life's problems. But she was neither unbalanced, nor sick, nor cynical. She was clearheaded, combative, thirsty for "nonconformist" happiness—and alone.*

As I now approach the most critical period of Gabrielle's life, that of her relationship with Christian and of the drama which grew out of it, I should indicate straightaway that I witnessed this only in the most indirect way. Up until 1966 I had seen a lot of Gabrielle. From 1966 to 1967 she devoted herself to the preparation for the *agrégation* in modern letters which she had decided to sit for, and, as is customary in preparing for such an examination, she reserved the major part of her time for her work. I remarked earlier that she had not originally foreseen where her university career would lead. When, on her return from Morocco, she had decided to continue her studies, she was in the typical—and I believe very common—situation of a young woman who, having married and had children early, feels the need to counter an experience which she considers "alienating," that of being a wife and mother, by achieving independence. She had passed her exams for this reason, probably without a job in view. But then she was swept away by her own success and progressively cleared the hurdles she had not anticipated. Following on the heels of her success with the *diplôme d'études supérieures*, she was encouraged to prepare for the *agrégation*. She passed in 1967 and under the best of circumstances (with honors in French). She had worked steadily for two years. And not without great reward. But here too, even if there are no grounds to go along with the myth and make too much of the fact that she prepared for this examination while raising two children alone, which, after all, must be the lot of many other young women (and Gabrielle had a salary from the IPES), it should be recognized that these conditions were hardly favorable and did impose additional hardship on her.

Fortunately she had many friends. Perhaps during this period of enforced retreat she had more than ever because of the contacts she made during her frequent visits to the faculty. Among her fellow students there were friends over whom she occasionally exercised a strange influence; some were very close to her, like Albert Roux, who remained her most faithful companion right up to the end. She had friends among the professors, especially the assistants in the French and linguistics departments who were her contemporaries in age and spirit and who very quickly came to think of her as one of them—Antoine Raybaud, Pierre Voltz, and later Claire Blanche. Effectively and fervently they helped "prepare" her for the examination and made her understand her potential.

More than all the others Antoine Raybaud showed her what she was made of. It seems to me that this had a lot to do with a certain concept of teaching which she made her own; and also in confirming and developing in her an uncompromising inclination not to separate culture from the problems of life itself. They shared a common tendency to literally "burn up" their lives, which by all accounts brought them close together. We can see today that it was during the course of these two years of intensive study at the faculty that Gabrielle assimilated the forms and principles of a new type of pedagogical relationship which depended on total reciprocal frankness and on the radical abolition of the hierarchical structure which was to a large extent the cause of her adventure; there is no doubt that her imprudence lay in transferring what she had experienced within the university to the lycée.

And she carried her enthusiasms into her home life too. The apartment building she lived in was surprisingly lively; the people from upstairs, the people from downstairs, the old lady next door, her children's classmates and their parents—because Gabrielle had a subtle art, or gift, of creating good neighborly relations; a "current" of fellow feeling was established between her and others which always surprised me and sometimes left me perplexed when I thought of all her other occupations. I believe that this situation was repeated in the apartment building she later moved to in Marseilles. Emphasizing this point is not without value, for it demonstrates that however real was a certain type of loneliness she experienced, the thing she missed the least was a "circle" of friends, as the presence of neighbors, friends, and colleagues, like Gilberte Thouvenet who was so close to her during the last months, shows.

When she passed the *agrégation* I was in Paris. She told me about the results immediately. She felt free and happy. She returned to the south of France in her Citroën *deux chevaux* with her little black cat mewing in a basket. She was setting out for a new life.

For Gabrielle

I don't know the precise sequence of events. Gabrielle herself told me certain things, Christian told me others, some I heard from a variety of witnesses. For the rest, like everyone else, I read the letters, the articles, the accounts, the reports. I have tried to get an idea of what happened through this complex mass of information, but I do not claim to know the whole truth. It seems to me today that what happened is relatively simple to sum up. Appointed to teach one of the large classes in a mixed lycée, Gabrielle gave herself unreservedly to her pupils, established the most personal ties with them, and in the context of these "exchanges" inspired a seventeen-year-old pupil to fall in love with her; and this love, aided by circumstances, particularly the general dispute which would end in the May 1968 explosion, grew into a real and lasting relationship that she intended to continue against all odds. It was inevitably a "scandalous" relationship when seen from the outside, but felt to be "innocent" and acceptable by those who experienced it directly—the interested parties and that whole body of witnesses, the class. In truth nothing was as unusual or as provocative as it may appear. Any professor who is not content with mediocrity, and who hopes to establish at least the minimum of communication with his students, has, one day or another, found himself in virtually the same situation. And this is particularly true of young women with male students. In short, Gabrielle merely "realized" an event which was already in the realm of possibility. Her error, if it was an error, was in not being aware of the danger that there was in making the leap, in a society which does not generally tolerate this kind of "switch," since *order* lies in not confounding reality with possibility.

This said, I know perfectly well that the plaintiffs in this affair presented the facts differently and spoke of the indisputable "deviation" of a minor, because this was the alleged offense. Their claim was founded on different facts: Christian, a second-year student, was only sixteen when the affair began, he was led to share Gabrielle's life and was thus removed from the family home, he was joined by her at various points, in particular during trips to Germany and Italy, and then, when others attempted to keep a distance between them (for example, by regis- tering him as a boarder at a school in Argelès), he made a number of escapes and disappeared several times, which gave the others the right to seek him out and protect him. I am wary of contesting these facts, which are probably all correct. I shall simply remark that all literature (which in this matter merely enlarges upon and illuminates life itself) reminds us that two people who love one another and are separated have a tendency to get back together at all costs, in the face of prudence and common sense, and to overcome by any possible means the barriers which have been placed between them. And I would add that love is always a "deviation" to a certain extent, since it means crisis, disorder, and the dispossession of oneself. But perhaps it was precisely because it was love that it could not be accepted, especially if there was the prospect of marriage, while a simple "fling" would have been tol- erated.

In this regard, I was struck that I very often heard of remarks made by Christian's parents (even in public statements) and by certain of their friends in which they used words like "bewitched," "hoodoo," "evil influence," "under a spell." In the Middle Ages people referred to love potions; doubtless they meant the same thing. It is true that the offense appears particularly serious when one of the two partners is fifteen years older than the other, and when the latter is a minor.

As it happens, at the age of seventeen Christian was like a man. I shall not dwell on the way he looked—a big, bearded boy. And I shall say little about his personality, which I barely knew. I shall, however, point out that as a militant from the extreme left (more particularly a member of what at that time was called the revolutionary Communist youth group) he had become by virtue of this an involved and responsible boy. It is very easy to say of a young man such as he that he is a "kid," but since May 1968 we have come to know that today's kids often see further than their fathers did. On the other hand, if one were to ask his parents' opinion of his personality, one would understand that he was a good intellectual "subject," and Gabrielle must very rapidly have become aware of this. I met him at the very moment the drama was in the making, during a meeting-debate on Czechoslovakia which was held in a progressive bookstore in Marseilles. He always seemed calm, master of himself, clearheaded, and deeply sincere. Of course he was still a "child," and perhaps it was in fact necessary to protect him from himself and to defend him. Was it protecting him to put him in a reeducative shelter on the advice of a magistrate, and then on that of a doctor in a clinical psychiatry cell; was it protecting him to subject him to injections and sleep cures? I only recall these facts because he himself accorded great importance to them and seems never to have accepted them.

On this subject I shall open a parenthesis to say that in actual fact the questions raised go very far beyond the limits of the case in question here. Françoise Parturier saw this very well in a remarkable article in Le Monde (October 10, 1969) entitled "Poor Parents," in which she showed that where the education of their children is concerned, families are extraordinarily unanimous in according absolute priority to all that is socially prudent and safe. "The sickness of the family is the fear of risk. Its credo is economy of the self, out of which comes the prohibition of all intense emotional activity. But I would like to know which science of human nature allows one to think that it is preferable to suffer for love rather than forfeit security. This is to decide that true love does not exist, and this is false and even stupid." And in order to show the real indomitable and decisive ill which lies behind this intolerance of love: "The truth of the matter is that once the child becomes a man, the parents cannot bear to lose him. It is terrible for the woman, who for fifteen years has been everything to her little boy, to watch this great love dissolve into affection. There is nothing to smile at because it is genuine suffering. If a mother is aware that she is jealous, she would not dare abandon herself to this jealousy, but if she is misleading herself and covering her passion with innocence, if she calls her anger duty, the child is lost and the persecution begins."

In fact, we can find a more rational approach to the phenomenon described here by drawing on what Wilhelm Reich called the theory of the "authoritarian family"—and if I mention Reich it is not because he is in fashion, but because on this point, as a Marxist and sexologist, he made a really unique contribution. The authoritarian family according to him is neither particularly reactionary nor middle-class, but any family where antisexual sentiments are in fact linked to the most severely repressed emotional relationships between its own members. "Whatever the class difference between families, they have this important possession in common—they have all been submitted to the same sexually moralizing atmosphere, an influence which does not run counter to class morality, but which co-exists with sexual morality. This attitude extends well beyond the lower-middle-class family, otherwise called the petit bourgeoisie, it applies equally to the upper classes and even to the working classes" (The Sexual Revolution). Reich demonstrates that such a family necessarily gives off a conservative sexual ideology and that by this same token it runs the risk of becoming "the principal breeding ground for the ideological atmosphere of all conservatism." Furthermore, he writes that the confusion between parental love and the authoritarian type of family organization leads to a repression of sexuality in the child and in the adolescent and slows the realization of this "unity of culture and of nature, of work and of love, of morality and sexuality for which humanity is perpetually searching" (The Function of the Orgasm). In Le Nouveau Monde Amoureux, Fourier had earlier referred to the "repressive politics of love which leads the society to poverty, deceit, and oppression." You will have understood why this digression does not seem totally useless to me, to

93

the extent that it is necessary to analyze the sociopsychological significance of the "security" and "protection" theory, particulary since the family in question here was politically as unconservative as possible.

(In reality, politics has nothing to do with the affair, and it is known that there are a number of Communists whose sexual morality is extreme. Forty years of Stalinist puritanism have not altered things and the few signs of change today are barely apparent.)

I shall be sorry if anyone takes what I have just written as an apology for Gabrielle Russier's behavior in regard to her student. In my opinion, this is the type of behavior that cannot be judged, that must first be thought of as a fact, a hard fact. Something has happened, it exists, pleasant or unpleasant, shocking or natural, it should not be the object of conjecture or generalization. But, alas, this is what happens constantly. To convince yourself of this fact, you merely have to recall the comments that were made here and there on the affair, or to reread some of the letters which were sent to different newspapers. In a case of this type everything happens as if the least attempt to "understand" assumes for some people the intolerable significance of a blanket justification, and, in addition, is an invitation to proselytize; to defend Gabrielle Russier is to invite all her colleagues to behave as she did and take her as their model. The rejoinder is inevitable: "What would happen if all teachers started sleeping with their pupils?" To which Michel Cournet has already supplied a reply: "In loving one of his students, in making him happy, in giving him more opportunities, a professor is only doing his duty." It seems to me that refusing to consider a given situation for itself alone and arguing on behalf of a generalization which masks the particular reality is to practice deception. Naturally it will be said that we are dealing with a question of professional "ethics," which must be respected even in individual cases, and even more so when the student is a "child" who has been *entrusted* to the teacher, as the public prosecutor said, for a precise and well-defined purpose. A not inconsiderable point of view, but it is hard to see why a society that looks benevolently upon a certain type of relationship such as may exist between a boss and his typist, a director and his secretary, a doctor and his patient, would necessarily compare the student-teacher relationship to that of a minister and his flock or a father and his children. One thing seems upsetting to me in any case: it is the declaration by the deputy public prosecutor who was called to prosecute Gabrielle, according to whom a professor may be compared to a public official ("I maintain that, like public officials, teachers should maintain a certain reserve."— *L'Express*, September 29, 1969). It was precisely against this concept of the "pedagogical relationship" based on authority that the whole May movement of 1968 rebelled and we know that all good teachers had taken the lead a long time before. As for Gabrielle, it is very clear that she was an excellent teacher, because she had abolished everything that could resemble the authoritarian transmission of knowledge between her and her students, because the type of communication she had established with them rested above all on a sort of experience (a common experience, protected from all elitist principles) and the immediate and real things in life, her life and theirs, which were considered as the only possible access to culture and knowledge.

That this is not without risk is only too evident. And if something must justify the particular situation in which Gabrielle found herself, it clearly lies in all the risks she had taken to "organize" and conceive of her class as she did. A famous work by Jean Cocteau, *Les enfants terribles*, has shown how fascinating and how deadly it can be to play the "game of truth" which is becoming popular with certain exclusive groups of adolescents—and a class is the most exclusive of groups, the furthest removed from the world of adults, the most sensitive to collective excitement. It is clear that the students in this mixed second-year class at the Lycée Saint-Exupéry had very quickly recognized one of their own in her whom they called "Gatito," a *deserter*, and that they were dazzled. "She was thirty years old, but she hardly seemed any older than us," said one of them, Florence. "She was tiny, very frail. She dressed and did her hair like us. Almost like a little pussycat. She had big black eyes. In her look you only saw her face, which was both burning and soft at the same time." A boy, Jacques, added, "With her everything became marvelous, fascinating. That's what's important. She took the stuffiness out of our school books and our minds. She loathed conformity, and helped us to be ourselves to an extraordinary degree" (*France-Soir*, September 28, 1969). They had never seen a teacher like her, and still today, whether their names are Claudette or Luc, Anne or Françoise (Françoise became Agnes for and *through* Gabrielle), the image of her that they keep in their memory can only be the jealously guarded picture of a woman who cannot be discussed in the language of adults.

Under these circumstances it is understandable that their parents were anxious and felt themselves cut off. Even felt their *raison d'être* to be vaguely threatened. And that, patient at first, they soon proved their need to act against the general "irregularity" which, it seemed to them, they saw developing in the class and which was "altering" their children, affecting their relationship with them. It appears that some of them wanted to lodge a complaint, but were dissuaded. One, a police officer, giving a very precise name to an indefinable offense, would have accused Gabrielle of organizing a "Communist cell" in her class. Others, fortunately, saw things for what they were, and through personal contact with her discovered and will never forget who this teacher really was. Because, basically, what Gabrielle was doing above all else was to continue to exist for her students once they had stepped over the classroom threshold. She joined them after school, went with them to the movies or the mountains, entertained them in her home. Obviously this is sufficient grounds for all manner of interpretations and rumors; it appears that when the magistrate and public prosecutor came to search her home one day, they looked everywhere for drugs and in an excess of professional zeal even tasted the most ordinary pill. What Gabrielle was actually doing was urging her pupils to self-examination; these confrontations probably did go quite a long way, possibly as far as intense dialogues on life, death, love, and sex, but that is precisely what the game of truth and the dizzying excitement of communication are about.

In this climate, "Chris" was a pupil like the others but destined to realize what the whole class was unconsciously leaning toward. Perhaps it was because he stood out among the boys as looking most like a man, perhaps he was simply the most in love. In any case, even if one imagines the sum of unconscious conflicts and secret jealousies to which his "promotion" must have given rise, the entire class identified with him and adopted the bond which linked him to Gabrielle. That is why it is not wrong to say that through Chris she married her class. This type of "delegation" of feelings is obviously characteristic of the adolescent world where affective transference takes place spontaneously, where individual tensions are absorbed into a collective symbol, and where love is respected above all. Doubtless this is the explanation for the Gabrielle-Christian cult which started then and will last forever.

Another important element was the events of May 1968. There could be a lot to say on this, but since Gabrielle's behavior does not seem to me to be in need of an excuse, it would be out of place to look for one in these events, and besides I do not want to get involved in a discussion about dates. I do not know if it was before, during, or after May that the relationship between Christian and Gabrielle crystallized. What I can say is that from that moment on they started being seen *publicly* and *freely* together. Particularly at the faculty, where they came quite often to take part in demonstrations. Which seemed to me to make sense. In fact, all of a sudden it seemed as if the events had given them some kind of *approbation*. What, until now, they had only been able to achieve with great difficulty and care suddenly they could achieve openly, they could "demonstrate" their love. Their attitude was legitimized and recognized. We know what May meant to the students as far as the liberation of desire, sexual demands, and the abolition of restrictions were concerned. "Take up your life." "Free your passion." "Let us live." "Someone is buying your happiness. Steal it back!" cried the walls of the Sorbonne. To listen was to be convinced. And if Gabrielle, who until then had scarcely been political (that is to say she held a middle-left position), then acquired a sort of heightened political conscience, it was clearly because she felt herself challenged by the events which swept her up, liberated by them from the "reality principle" in the Freudian sense of the expression. It therefore seems possible to me to say that May '68 was the source of an extraordinary "acceleration" in her adventure with Christian and through this we can more easily understand future developments (since the most noteworthy or "scandalous" episodes took place in the months that followed). On the other hand we would not be wrong in assuming that in a strange way it was her *lot* to be ahead of the spirit of May 1968, to be May's premature child. One thing is certain, she was made to pay very dearly for May, because we know, once the threat had been removed, the distaste with which a whole layer of society denounced the disorder and "debauchery" that had been acted out in universities and lycées for a number of weeks. They had to produce a proof of this. They held an irrefutable one. The magistrate stood by to make an example of her.

I do not know how to explain the reason things grew

more complicated during the summer of 1968 and the period which followed. Gabrielle would not give up. Was she fighting for her love, struggling against the whole society; had she simply decided to challenge Christian's parents right to the end, to "conquer" them, despite the very cooperative attitude she had initially shown them? In any case, the situation in which she was placed bore a certain "dynamic" to the quasi-inescapable consequences. I saw less and less of her at this time; but all the same I did meet her on occasion to discuss her candidacy and eventual nomination as an assistant in linguistics on the faculty (a plan which was the cause of all sorts of obscure maneuvers by the university administration). Each time she was in a different mood. It was clear that she was living through an ordeal and, as I have said, went from high to low. One day, when she was still living in Aix, I found her in a veritable state of crisis and she showed me a plywood board which hid an enormous hole in the door of her apartment that Christian had made trying to break through—in passing we should note that this is proof that sometimes she must have tried to discourage him before events took their turn (and that she was therefore not as "obstinate" as people often wanted to imagine her). Another day—it was in a café—she brought out of her purse a photograph of Christian and showed it to me with an astonishing expression of happiness. Occasionally she sent me little notes which she signed amusingly "Dyana Rossa," an allusion to her car—a Dyane—her red turtle, which at that time played a strange and complex role in her life, particularly in her travels and dealings with the police.

The complaint had been lodged and the police were already on her trail. I only came to know this later. In August 1968 Gabrielle had moved, leaving Aix without warning to set up house near her lycée and near Christian in an apartment perched high in the enormous Résidence Nord, in the Saint Antoine district of Marseilles with a view of the distant sea.

She was jailed for the first time in December 1968 for five days, at the end of an escapade with Christian. She returned to Les Baumettes in April 1969, for eight weeks this time.

Fortunately a whole movement in Gabrielle's favor grew at the faculty, particularly in the linguistics department, where Jean Stefanini, her former professor, had never ceased to watch out for her welfare. Nevertheless, she served her eight weeks. She was set free on June 14.

Some letters from her made me sense her progressive moral and physical deterioration. It was a strange feeling to open those envelopes which bore the number 59.264 and to unfold the pages marked with the rectangular censor's stamp. The last one I received (which you will read here) revealed through its trembling writing, uneven appearance, broken sentences, and garbled message profound torment. Gabrielle was very far from the "good sport" frame of mind in which she had first faced her new experience. She was broken. And that is certainly how she looked to me when I saw her again. A few days after she was set free she came to the faculty at Aix where I had made a date to see her; I found her, with her big dark glasses covering her eyes, sitting peculiarly in front of a door, cowering in a corner as if she did not dare to go in or cross the hall. When she took off her glasses in the little Pont de l'Arc restaurant where I took her, I did not recognize her. Haggard, pale, undone, thin, she made me understand what the expression "to be a shadow of oneself" means. In addition, she glanced constantly from left to right and behind her, as if she felt she was being spied upon and hunted down. She barely ate, seemed to breathe with difficulty, spoke in a very weak voice. I tried to listen to what she was saying, but in fact all my attention was in my look, fixed on this *unknown* young woman on the other side of the table. She talked to me about the conditions of her detention. I shall not go into these matters because I think the letters you will find in this book say enough. But on that day I saw what prison can do.

Here I shall stop again. I know that someone will point out that I am falling into the black romanticism of jails and that it is not necessary to emphasize Gabrielle's own experience to show that she was crushed by two months' internment. But there was the painter, the little addict with whom Gabrielle became friendly, here is her testimony, I have not changed one word of it.

"When Gabrielle arrived among us she was plunged without transition into a squalid world, ruled by an ironlike discipline which was, however, incapable of fighting the spitefulness, jealousy, and vulgarity that dominate the prison world. The first and the worst of the humiliations Gabrielle faced was to strip entirely naked in front of the others so that her clothes and underwear could be thoroughly searched. Never in all her life had Gabrielle felt such shame, but no one took

the least notice." I am interrupting this report a minute because, as I was transcribing those lines, I suddenly heard the poem, which she knew well, that Apollinaire wrote when he went into La Santé.

> *Avant d'entre dans ma cellule*
> *Il a fallu me mettre nu*
> *Et quelle voix sinistre ulule*
> *Guillaume qu'est-tu devenue?**

"She had been assigned to cell number thirteen, the one I occupied on the ground floor of the women's quarters. When the heavy door closed behind her Gabrielle Russier had even lost her name. She was no more than registration number 59.264. When she joined the others in the courtyard for the daily walk from two to four o'clock, no one yet knew the reason for her presence at Les Baumettes. Since her hair was cut very short, tomboy style, the most spiteful of the prisoners immediately spread the rumor that she was a lesbian. Horrible comments were made. Gabrielle, pale as death, had to listen to them without saying anything. She looked like a frightened kid faced with the ferocity of adults. Each time someone accused her so as to add to her humiliation, Gabrielle replied with sweetness and intelligence. What made the guards furious was that she never expressed herself coarsely, yet she could not have escaped learning the prison language. From morning to night she was forced to listen to the revolting obscenities our guards addressed to her. In the most

* Before I went into my cell/I had to strip naked/And whose sinister voice echoed/Guillaume, what has become of you?

unpleasant terms they jeered at the pure, deep love she still felt for Christian despite all that had happened. She who had spent her whole life among books went to find consolation in the library of Les Baumettes. One day when Gabrielle had taken me there to introduce me to certain authors a guard come toward her and said, 'What good is this to you? You're nothing more than a rag. Your life's finished' " (France-Dimanche, September 9, 1969).

Since I am on the subject of prisons, I should like to say what I think of the repressive apparatus which was brought to bear against Gabrielle. Twice an examining magistrate sentenced her to preventive detention after having found her guilty; the second time it lasted for two months. I don't know this magistrate. I read somewhere that he has the reputation of being particularly "upright and scrupulous," that he has a certain southern affability, that he is a big amateur yachting enthusiast. Surely a balanced man who understands the demands of his profession and remains "deaf to any condemnation from the street." It is said that Gabrielle made him lose patience several times (and this seems utterly likely). While he was threatening her with arrest if she did not reveal where Christian could be found, she even challenged him, "All right then, arrest me!" But is it the role of a magistrate to lose patience and take the accused up on his word? Should he use preventive detention for anything other than to ensure the manifestation of truth? Or again, was there reason to consider that Gabrielle was really dangerous like a big-time criminal, and that it was necessary to keep her out of the way in order to protect Christian? Or to think that she intended to escape when she had answered all the summonses she received? The official line is that she had to tell where Christian was each time he disappeared; and that they had to be sure she no longer had the physical possibility of "deviating" him; and, moreover, that the pursuit of the inquiry required that she be put away. It seemed more straightforward to me simply that once a bond of cause and effect had been established between Christian's disappearances and Gabrielle's acts, she served as a hostage each time he "stirred." Preventive detention, which I believe I have heard described as something that should be used only with great care and in extreme cases, was used here as a means of pressure and coercion on a suspect who would not yield, and who was given the following alternatives: either deliver Christian (and renounce him) or go to prison—love or Les Baumettes. Since she was proud, it was also necessary to break her spirit.

In fact it is possible that the magistrate thought he was doing his job, which raises another question, why a magistrate? And why justice? It is difficult for me to take up this point without talking about Christian's parents who set this "justice" in motion. I am reluctant to do so because I have known them for a long time and always considered them as friends and political comrades. I would even say that as Communists the sympathy they exhibited for the Italian Communist party position often seemed positive to me. That they had shown sufficiently clear "leftist" principles in May 1968 neither surprises me nor does it reveal any contradiction in their attitude (as shortsighted journalists have attempted to point out), but seems to be perfectly understandable. What I have not been able to explain to myself, and I say this very plainly, is that, being what they are, they did all the same lodge a complaint against a person who was not only their son's friend, but also their colleague and former student, with all the consequences that this action would bring upon both this person and their son, and that in addition they sought to have her removed "by the administration" at all costs. I know very well that they had their reasons, which I have already discussed, and that they must have considered them sufficient. But I hope no one will ask me to put myself in their place. To the type of question which goes, "Do you know what you would have done if you had a son of that age who . . . who . . . ?" I see only one possible answer, the one that Emile Breton gave in La Marseillaise (October 12, 1969): "I don't know what I would have done, but I do know very well what I would not have done." In my article in Le Monde I wrote, "As leftists they should have known what a destructive machine the bourgeois police apparatus and justice is." That sentence was not intended to be insulting or polemical. It merely expressed a general sentiment. I know perfectly well that certain people are ready to reply, "So, liberal, if someone steals your car, you would not complain to the bourgeois law?" The problem is that in this case it was not a car, and other things were at stake. Moreover, I am not saying that Gabrielle had to be mortally wounded by the repressive, pitiless wheels of justice, as the facts have so tragically shown, but that *this was in the realm of possibility. And that the distinguishing feature of leftist thought seems to me not to put confidence in a legal order where, as in a case like this, police action is inseparable from the defensive and repressive system of the society in question. To consider justice in the abstract and not in the context of its social effect is an error which can prove costly, as we have seen. One day I heard someone say quite openly, "What dumbfounded people about this affair was that the young man's parents were professors, university graduates, involved intellectuals; if they had been shipowners, businessmen, farmers, or I don't know what, things would have seemed much less surprising and there would not have been such an outcry." It is a remark that I shall take to heart.*

I saw Gabrielle for the last time on June 23, 1969. I had decided to introduce her to the "other side's" attorney, not because I wanted to reach some extralegal agreement, but simply because Maître Christian Grisoli was one of my oldest friends and it seemed possible to me to put this meeting in the context of personal relations; I felt that in seeing and listening to Gabrielle, Christian Grisoli would understand who she was and would get a clearer idea of his responsibilities. He would at least see for himself that she was neither the abductress nor the devourer of children he had perhaps imagined. The meeting took place, relaxed and simple. It is a strange and troubling memory today because Christian Grisoli is dead now too (recently carried off by a pitiless disease) and at the time that I write these lines the memory of the conversation between those two doomed people in the half-light of the big office lit by a low lamp comes back to me like a distant dream. It was evening. It was pouring rain in Marseilles. Gabrielle had come in my car accompanied by Claudette, one of her students, who had to leave us on the way. When the visit was over she got back into the car without being able to avoid the downpour completely: water was streaming off her, her hair was stuck to her temples. We drove through Marseilles lit with neon lights, dodging through the crazy traffic, to the sound of the windshield wipers. I left her off at the Résidence Nord, her home, around eight o'clock. I opened the door and she got out into the rain which was still falling.

Why did Gabrielle Russier commit suicide? The question will remain unanswered. Yet I consider that if no one has the right to surmise the reason, it does seem absolutely legitimate to make a statement on the conditions which permitted this suicide. I place the state of least psychic resistance in which Gabrielle found herself at the end of her long imprisonment, and particularly on the eve of the appeal, in the first rank of these conditions. On this point the witnesses agree and abound. All those who saw her on July 10 confirm that at the end of her trial she had received with extraordinary relief and a feeling of veritable liberation the sentence which condemned her to one year's suspended imprisonment, subject to amnesty. She was out of the woods, she regained her confidence, she cabled her attorney, "Thank you. Long live the sun. Antigone." The following day, on learning of the decision which had thrown everything back into the balance, she broke down and was overcome by an anguish that would never leave her. Here again the testimony is precise, legion, and convincing. The need for a rest in the Pyrenees is one fact among others. But it is essential to consider that this new and reinforced anguish took over from a torment that had never ceased troubling Gabrielle for months and which had little by little undermined her psyche. This will be understood most clearly by reading the letters sent to her friends and family beginning in May 1969; it is because they are the diary of a torment and by this token bear the burden of proof that they are brought together here. Proof of what? Of the unconscious feeling that Gabrielle had to be the object of "persecution." I do not say that this feeling led her straight to suicide, but I maintain that it created sufficient insecurity within her so that the doubt, panic, and disgust proved fatal. Her "adventure" had already been difficult enough to live through, the intervention of justice had already sufficiently distorted her senses whatever the issue of the appeal would be, the return before the tribunal meant crossing a certain threshold of irreparability. And here I leave the word to an observer, Jean-René Vernes, who seems to me to have gotten closer to the truth than anyone. "In order for a woman to be able to accept an open conflict with the law, as Gabrielle Russier did and under the conditions in which she did it, she must already feel herself driven to the limits of despair. Young love fed to the contestants of a trial is already lost love. It is condemned to watch its purity being destroyed, an inner purity perhaps, but one without which it cannot survive. It is here that the law in its cruelty helps no one, neither the parents, nor the lovers, nor even, in the final analysis, the public prosecutor. Justice assumes a rigidity which the complex workings of the human heart find hard to accept. Because no one escapes this law which can only be convinced and purified through the acceptance of proof. But here one cannot accept the renunciation of the person one loves and in whom one believes because in so doing one discovers little by little the interior necessity, one cannot accept it without losing oneself through brute force and injury."

If we accept the above, we must ask, was there brute force and injury? No, there was simply justice! But what is this justice which, on the evening of July 10, decided with cold determination to "reverse" the law of amnesty declared by the president of the Republic on the occasion of his taking office? Because, as is perfectly clear to everyone, if the public prosecutor of Aix through the intermediary of the prosecutor and his deputy in Marseilles appealed the sentence, it was because he considered that Gabrielle had not received sufficient punishment, and that it was necessary to obtain a new sentence, harsh enough to be exempted from the amnesty. In this case, she would really have been *punished;* in particular she could have been officially penalized by her profession, the thing she dreaded above all else. The deputy wrote, "An inscription on her police record was needed so as to facilitate disciplinary action and remove her from her post" (*L' Express,* September 20, 1969). Therefore the magistrates did what *they had to.* People wondered if they were acting on advice from the university or academic authorities. But no, there was nothing. No sign. Telephone calls? Possible meetings? Pure speculation. The distinguishing feature of the middle-class society's security system is that it leaves no trace of having been used. It literally has no material location. The notables of a town of 100,000 inhabitants are a part of provincial folklore; but the reality of their power and their solidarity has neither place, nor name, nor face. One can act as spokesman for them all. The public prosecutor announced that he needed no one to help him make his decision and that he made it in his soul and in his conscience. This is what is astonishing, because if taken at face value one would think that the decision to appeal made with no precedent a few hours after the sentence was pronounced was an act of reflex rather than of reflection. But so be it, soul and conscience!

In the matter which concerns us three unwritten laws were brought into effect with uncommon force and efficiency:

A teacher does not sleep with his pupils.
A woman does not have an affair with a boy fifteen years her junior.
One does not defy the law and escape punishment.

I have already discussed the first point, I shall not return to it. I would simply remind you that the deputy public prosecutor did not hesitate to state that in Gabrielle's case the fact that she was a teacher made her offense far more serious (while, on the contrary, it obviously explained everything). As for the second point, it has been said and repeated a hundred times over that in the case of the deviation of minors, the French penal system—and in this it faithfully reflects the customs of the country—treats women more severely than men (because if the minor is a consenting female the prosecution is dropped). But what has not been sufficiently emphasized is the kind of truly terrifying hatred which a woman who is accused of seducing an adolescent attracts. She has "treated herself" to a young boy; she has given in to a cynical whim; her behavior is inescapably shameful. The ferocious antifeminism which triggers this reaction is even more odious because it is purely the expression of a social practice. In fact, when these things happen in literature everything is different. If Madame de Warens has a weakness for little Jean-Jacques (fourteen years her junior), Madame de Rênal for Julien, the Countess Sanseverina for Fabrice, Phaedra for Hippolytus, Martha for François, Léa for Chéri, everything is normal, it is a question of perfectly standard literary situations, admitted and recognized as such. Now—another little parenthesis—the Russier affair took place in a world in which literature holds a certain position, yet this was not taken into account. On this subject we would benefit by reading a letter addressed to *Le Monde* by Monsieur Philippe Berthier: "We urge young people to allow themselves to be transported by literary masterpieces, but they may not imitate them on pain of social disapproval and unanimous disclaim."

Gabrielle had, in fact, confused literature with life, and she never wanted to admit her mistake. That is the third point. The challenge. The stubbornness. The insolence. Here too the deputy spoke. He said that if she had made "honorable amends" things could have been different. But then she never did make honorable amends. She never did excuse herself. She did not say that she had made a mistake and that she would not start over again. It is even said that when the sentence was passed on July 10, she looked as though she wanted to "win," to have the last word, and that was not to the public prosecutor's taste. Right up until the end she wanted to assert that she had done nothing wrong—which was her deepest conviction, but which she was asked to keep to herself. In sum, not only had she violated the two unwritten laws discussed above, but to this double transgression she had added an even more serious sin, that of not accepting the rules of the game, and this is why she was "guilty." And it is why she was broken. Because in cases like this one is always broken by society, which is the stronger. Shrewder people will go about challenging society obliquely. Gabrielle faced it head on. It seems that in certain freewheeling and sexually liberated Parisian circles, she was regarded with a sort of pity tinged with condescension. It would have been so easy for her to live out her little drama if she had known how to go about it, it's done every day in the better world. But no, she had to be headstrong, she had to play Antigone, she had to reply, discuss, reason, instead of keeping quiet and allowing herself to be forgotten. Yet a long time ago Tartuffe whispered:

> *Le scandale du monde est ce qui fait l'offence*
> *Et ce n'est pas pecher que pecher en silence.*

She should have remembered.

There was no money grabbing or profiteering here. There was simply something extraordinarily naïve and clumsy that could be called love, provocation, or unawareness, but which at the outset was not soiled by suspicion. In the eyes of those who came to hear about it, it was far more serious—a real change was taking place, and when part of an edifice is changed the whole building is immediately threatened. It was therefore necessary to act.

After Gabrielle's death everything started again, the newspapers, the noise. The drama played an extraordinarily revelatory role. What had been only a matter of some confusion to the public all of a sudden grew quite unexpectedly. Again there were headlines, sensational articles, exclusive photos (for example there was the extremely curious one from *Ici Paris*, that old rag, showing a bearded young man, his eyes hidden by a black rectangle, with the following caption: "This young man is *not* Christian, but it is a student of the same age with a beard like his who *could be* Christian"). Then the last barriers of decency fell. Reports followed inquiries. Mistakes were rife. The sensation-seeking press opened its columns wide to them. On the whole the papers presented a version of the events which favored Gabrielle. However, Jean Cau, doubtless with a taste for paradox and independence, wrote a sadly offensive piece about her in *Paris-Match*. It was his right, but it seems to me that there is a certain tone one should not adopt in the face of death and pain. To pass on. A whole sociological study could be made through the articles it prompted of the effect the Russier affair had on the general public. I shall take this opportunity to backtrack and say that as far as I am concerned the press played a very well defined role in Gabrielle's despair and demoralization. What happened after her death had already taken place once before, but at that time she was present to read the papers and see her story reflected by them, distorted, misrepresented, or simply exposed. And I do not see how such a deprivation of a person's most intimate feelings could fail to unbalance even the most stable individual, how the image of his love and troubles reflected by the world outside would not add irreparably to his loneliness and confusion. Less and less belongs to him alone, even facts which he believed to be "nonnegotiable"; from now on he is only what others make of him. The press should consider this and like Cocteau's mirrors would do well to reflect further. But it fulfills its function—it informs, it transforms. In its own way each daily, each weekly, each monthly, each radio station produces the best possible edition without looking ahead or behind, for by definition "news" is neither to-morrow nor yesterday.

But the press is not everything. To understand the prodigious effects of Gabrielle's drama on the individual mind perhaps one day it will be necessary to consider all the letters that strangers wrote about her, for her and against her. Some were found in the "mailbag" section of newspapers, we heard them read by the armload over Radio Monte Carlo. After the publication of a short article, I received astonishing quantities, people speaking, questioning, denouncing, faultfinding, suddenly confessing their own problems, reliving their distress, settling old ac-counts with justice, abruptly coming out of themselves, projecting themselves by mail into another's unhappiness. And then there were all those who were more immediately affected, more secretly, more darkly, for whom Gabrielle had become a sister and a companion, who recognized themselves in her. If ever the adjective "concerned" had a meaning, it applied incomparably to all of them.

There were other less secret, more strident repercussions. I have not until now mentioned the backwash which was produced by a supplementary affair that was attached to the main one, but I shall say a few words here. Gabrielle, as I have already indicated, was to have been named an assistant to the linguistics faculty of letters at Aix. Her nomination had been postponed in 1968 for reasons that were not clear. In 1969, in the thick of her troubles, her candidacy was again brought up by the French department. The temporary faculty council turned her down by a small majority; certain of its members, informed of the charges against her, did not consider it wise to give her their votes. It was their inalienable right but it was quite evident that, in doing so, they did not show themselves insensible to certain criteria which have less to do with the candidate's competence than with his private life. Now, since she had simply been accused but not found guilty she had the right to a maximum of guarantees. This vote caused a lot of trouble on the day after her death. The students mobilized and led a vigorous campaign against the council; moral order and the "repressive" university system were held responsible for Gabrielle's death. (The Jean Verdeil affair—the professor from Nîmes who was imprisoned for having smoked "hash" with a few young people—confirmed their suspicions.) This offensive lasted two months. It was violent, and undiscriminating, the Maoist and leftist proletarian university and high school students having taken over the direction of the movement not only at the faculty but at the Lycée Nord de Marseille where Gabrielle had left her mark. She rapidly became a saint and "Maoist heroine"; if it had been possible to raise her effigy and march it through the streets, I think that would have been done. A curious posthumous destiny which has often puzzled me because I never thought of Gabrielle as "Chinese" or even really revolutionary. I believe however that the students in question were not mistaken when they said that her eviction was political. They endowed this word with a meaning which far outstrips the ordinary sense of the term, but I think that this meaning is finally admissible. For a long time their action seemed dangerously intemperate to me, and without doubt it was, but today, as I reread one of the tracts which they distributed, I find it is one of the most beautiful homages that have been made to Gabrielle. I am transcribing this document without changing anything.

A TEACHER UNLIKE THE OTHERS

She was not a teacher like the rest of them. She didn't crush us with her authority. She became our friend and discussed all life's problems with us. She treated us as equals and it was in this context that she could have an affair with one of her students.

But it was in May 1968 that she really showed whose side she was on. She did not hesitate to denounce the tactics of the administration and reactionary professors who were trying to destroy the lycéean movement. She also sided with the workers, actively taking part in the collection of funds for the strikers on the lycée staff. The bourgeoisie will not forgive her. The teaching body does not allow one of its own to destroy the image of the matchless and indisputable teacher. It is for this reason she was going to be excluded by them. An affair with one of her students and look at all the fuss it created.

But why so much relentlessness? When relationships of this kind exist in many lycées and are discreetly hushed up, why so much fuss about Gabrielle? Because since May the bourgeoisie's power, which in lycées is assumed by the teachers, has been more and more shaky. In these circumstances they can no longer allow a teacher, one of the agents of authority, to go over to the enemy, over to the camp of the students who are in revolt; that is why they wanted to make an example of Gabrielle Russier when school started in 1969.

But if Gabrielle died for having come over to our camp, let us be ready to follow her example and to fight against all authoritarian and decadent relations between teachers and pupils in lycées.

> The Maoists of the Proletarian Left
> Lycée Nord, Marseilles

I don't know what Gabrielle would have thought of this text and of the way in which her cause was defended. There is little doubt that she would not have liked all the fuss and violence. But, on reflection, the violence she suffered was much more powerful than all the violence her drama has inspired. Sometimes it seems to me that she would not have understood what happened after her death any better than she understood what was happening during the last year of her short life. In her letters and conversation she often referred to a character who appears to have obsessed her—Camus' Meursault. She was "the stranger" in her way. She identified with him before the judges, she felt the hatred, the fury and the stupidity growing around her, she went as far as death. She never knew what was happening to her or why. She never saw that she was being blamed less for the things she had done than for the manner in which she did them, denounced by everyone for her behavior and unacceptable to society such as it is. Which is why she lost. When I think of her today, I don't know why but I hear this line by Pavese:

Verra la morte e avra tuoi occhi.

(Death will come and it will have your eyes.)

Letters of
Gabrielle Russier

March 8, 1968

Dear Françoise*

I must finish up what I have begun in Marseilles. It will take another year or two.

Yes, it is paradise, more and more . . .

Dangerous too. And exhausting. But now I can't give it up, I no longer have the right to do so.

This training period has its difficulties because the classes react badly. And then I'm something of an accomplice in spite of myself. But I'm happy back in the classroom, in my place at last.

Yesterday I dragged my whole world from Marseilles to Aix to see a poetic dramatization of Baudelaire done by Raybaud and some friends. My kids were happy. Tomorrow a skiing trip.

And there's also the discovery of poverty when I visit my students' homes
of ignorance
of the parents' courage

G

*Her childhood friend, an assistant in the faculty of letters at Rouen.

August 4, 1968

Dear old friend

No, I haven't received your letter before last, so I don't understand very much in the latest one about your vacation plans. I get the idea you had a great time in Rouen, but that's only reading between the lines. I should like you to tell me. So much has happened that I've forgotten the half of it. Certain images remain in my mind; glimpses of crowds, of faces, of people who gave me their hands in the demonstrations.

Glimpses too of a plot which is building up and which could go a long way. I am back from Italy. Set out for Sicily, but never got there for reasons I can't go into in a few words. A long stay in Rome. Now I have to find myself an apartment and move in. The children are arriving on the 9th and leaving again for camp.

If the idea appeals to you, take the Mistral and come down to be with me, to chat and work, to help me set up my new home. I'll help you get acquainted with the back streets of Marseilles and those of my pupils who have not yet left for vacation, or have already returned.

I am suggesting this hesitantly, not daring to believe that you might accept. All the same, you would make me very happy. If you do decide, let me know quickly.

I'm writing you stretched out in the sun, which is why my writing is scrawled. I'm a little sad because I have the feeling that the vacation is over.

If you don't come, tell me how you are, what you're up to, what you are enjoying.

I would have so much to tell you that can't be written about—too long and too complicated.

I think we could have a good time together because I'm getting more and more as I was in Duruy. It's my students' fault, they've made me fifteen years old again. (Minus the silliness, I think.)

I'm ending my letter here because I would just ask you to come again.

With love

Gabrielle

Monday, end of October, 1968

Dear, dear Albert*

I can write you, you can write me, it's over.

Or nearly

Only that "nearly" helps me to go on living, and also the words from people who have understood; your words, you.

I am on a long leave for nervous depression, but it's really because the principal doesn't want to see me anymore.

I can't stand Aix any longer, or the faculty, but with you perhaps it would be all right. I must get used to it.

I hope the exam went off OK despite us.

Tell me when you will be there, or if you can, come see us. I'll be here until All Saints', except on Saturday afternoon. And if you have work, I'll help you in a short time. I miss the lycée and I don't feel like reading anymore.

With love

* Her schoolfellow and friend.

Grazie
and everything I don't know how to say.

G

[TO RAYMOND JEAN] *January 8, 1969*

Your card gave me real pleasure. It's pretty. It symbolizes many of the things I like, and therefore is permanently fixed to the windshield of a red and, from now onward, famous Dyane.

Despite the knocks, despite the times, despite human unkindness.

I haven't forgotten anything.

Not the station at Narbonne, nor Eluard's record, nor the discovery of a young woman with short hair who will have brought another young woman with short hair back to life.

Which means freedom and happiness for many people today.

Who is the author?

G

[TO FRANÇOISE] *February 18, 1969*

Dear Fanchon

If I could explain to you everything that's happened since October you wouldn't blame me for not writing.

Unfortunately, it's impossible to do so by letter, it would take forty pages. It sounds like something out of San Antonio and Racine, perhaps it will end up as an item in the newspaper.

So pray to Saint Anthony and Saint Christopher to protect us. I say this in all seriousness. I'm asking you to do it.

I can't explain to you. The people to whom I told this story thought I was raving, but the facts have proved them wrong. Don't get upset. But you who have faith, pray that we are spared the massacre. We have escaped it a dozen times already, but the rock of Sisyphus is still here; we have to roll it back up the slope, to endure new catastrophes.

I hope you will write me. But watch out, my mail is possibly being read.

I hope you will come at Easter. In theory it should all be over by then and we shall be out of the woods.

Then I'll show you the real Marseilles, and lots of great people, and the real life and two lucky cats—one tiny little one who won't grow and a fat black one with a white tie.

With love

Gabrielle

[TO RAYMOND JEAN]   *Saturday, March 14, 1969*

Dear R. J.

Friday if you like. I'll park at the side of the Rotonde around 3 P.M.

Would be very happy to chat with you, and also to get

away from my troubles a bit. The infernal machine is still going. Last week a thirteen-year-old kid, the brother of a student who has become a friend, was drowned. The girl is very upset.

Until I see you, sadly because it's a long time and it's raining,

but always affectionately

G

PS: Thank you for having done something,
for having understood,
for helping me to survive

Dyana Rossa

[TO MADAME GILBERTE T.*] *Tuesday before Easter,* 1969

I shall not send you flowers because you're going away and because certain gestures are intimidating. But I wanted to tell you that the walk revived me a little at a time when I felt myself cracking. I rediscovered the trees and the sea and perhaps my confidence too. Thank you for having brought me all that.

Good luck with the administrative steps you have to take—don't be too angry with me for having appointed you ambassadress of charm.

Best

G. N.

* A neighbor and colleague at the Lycée Nord de Marseille.

[TO MADAME GILBERTE T.] *April* 1969

It's late. I've been invited to dinner at Aix. Attached is a letter for the principal with a request for Vanves, and the copy of the letter to the rector. I too only bring you complications and problems. I hope (and I believe) the time will come when I shall be able to give you a real smile, and no more complaining, and the affection that I feel but can't express, whether it is because the misery has gotten the upper hand or because, like today, all the red tape and administrative fussing have taken up where my other troubles left off.

Thank you for helping me keep a hold on the helm when I lost strength

and, come what may

Best wishes

G. N.

[TO MADAME GILBERTE T.'S MOTHER, AGED EIGHTY-SIX] *Saturday, April* 1969

Dear Madame

Various administrative formalities and a violent migraine stopped me from coming over to get news of you this morning as I had intended.

I hope that miserable depression has lifted, and that your weekend in the country will take your mind off it so that you will come back wreathed in smiles. You will be with people who love you, and I hope you won't forget that those who remain in Marseilles love you too, and wish you a happy life.

Don't make problems for yourself. Remember that summer is not far away, that life is not as monotonous as you think, and that happy times always follow sad times.

Very best wishes

G.N.

April 27, 1969

My dear Albert

I hope my absence from the Raybaud course and the arrival of individuals who decided to attend did not upset you too much. I am very sorry, but since I was going to the course, they imagined that I must be seeing Chris there! Can I ever say enough to you about steering clear of unpleasant company—you see where it leads!

In short, here I am inside again, but I'm writing as quickly as possible to tell you not to worry. I'm well and in very good company. I would be very happy to get news of you, you can write me "freely" at the above address. Send me some postcards or reproductions, nothing could make me happier. Later, I shall perhaps call on you for some material help, to bring me parcels for example. Perhaps you could telephone the SNES* to bring them up to date, and the others too. I hope you're continuing to teach with your usual serenity and that your students will

* National Syndicate for Secondary Education.

give you less trouble than mine. If you have time to write me, tell me about Greece. You have always been our faithful Hermes, everyone knows that right now, but what is the Greek name for the god who takes parcels to prisoners? Perhaps there weren't any prisons in Greece. In any event it was simpler: they put people in a hole and stopped talking about them.

Mercury, then, glide in peace (and move around for me since the red tortoise has been immobilized). Look at the trees in my place, say hello to the setting sun, and don't forget what I said in the letter you read at the Rotonde, "I shall listen to music and the music will no longer be sad, etc." Don't worry, remember the agreement and Eluard's verses. The little Saint Bernard sends you a kiss.

Gatito

PS: Chloë will not allow herself to be suffocated by the water lily and long live Boris Vian.

2ND PS: Send me some stamped envelopes, please.

End of April 1969

Dear Madame

Gilberte, if you'll allow me to call you that after a memorable picnic.

I am writing you in the hope that you have not been too worried about me, and to ask you to act as my interpreter for Madame R. because she reads French badly and therefore I can't write her. Above all I should like everyone to be assured that I'm all right, and for Joël to be told that I send him a kiss and that I'm very well, which is true. I think Madame R. will be able to keep him as long as I stay here. Tell her also not to inform my father for the time being, and only to do so if my stay is prolonged. On the other hand, she has the addresses of people in Aix whom she should warn, whether it is through Albert Roux or by some other means. Perhaps someone should tell the SNES about it, in case they need me.

Above all Madame R. must tell everyone who comes to get news of me that I am well, that I'm eating, sleeping, and resting, and that I'm with two very pleasant girls (whom I already knew and with whom they put me back). This could go on for a very long time but there is absolutely no need to worry. Just to let people know. They can write me "freely" and I shall be very happy to receive mail, so Madame R. can give out my address. I'd like people to send me postcards. I am only allowed to see my lawyer and my family, but later I shall perhaps ask Madame R. to bring me some laundry, which is permitted. She can come to the door.

Tell her to take good care of Joël (and Frotadou*) and to water the rose tree. Joël should also be asked to write to Valérie from time to time: La Joie de Vivre, Château de Verdun, 73, Cruet. Forgive me for bothering you with all this. And above all, don't worry. At the moment the only problems are material: I have the two keys to the mailbox. The car is in the garage for repairs. And though the May rent has not been paid, the taxes have.

* The little household cat.

Apart from that everything is for the best in the best of all possible worlds.

Out in the courtyard I have gotten to know "Satan." A really weird little hippie. There are all types, but it is not as bad as in novels and certainly much easier to bear than the psychiatric clinic or hospital. I was never able to stay more than three days in the clinic but it is very different here because once you're in your cell you're perfectly free (Yes!). I'm a little tired because we talked until late yesterday, but tomorrow is Sunday and after mass I'll take a little siesta before the outing in the courtyard . . . then crocheting or knitting, reading, discussion.

I should like to succeed in making you laugh, so I'll be forgiven for having given you trouble, and making you go to Madame R.'s at the risk of scandalizing the neighborhood. But I know your respectable demeanor and little red shoes will protect you from all scandalmongering.

Say hello to our dear pharmacist from me. He would be useful here to unclog the johns and make up the beds. I must say that bunk beds are perfect for trapeze and abdominal exercises.

Outside there are low-income housing projects where people are imprisoned in their routine. The advantage we have over them is in knowing we are imprisoned, and also in knowing that real life does go on.

It's easy to philosophize here. Tempting even. This place is like a boarding school or a convent. It's better—and less dangerous—than what they inflicted at the other.

You'll see, one day we shall climb aboard *The Misunderstood* and sunbathe, and it will be like that afternoon you took me to the shore.

Tell your mother that I'm resting in the country and that I send her my best wishes. I hope she's in good spirits.

I'm ending this epistle here. Don't reply, you have enough to do for me with Madame R. and the SNES.

Make it known at the lycée that I have not taken Christian away, which they may start thinking again, and that I haven't seen him for three months!

Hoping to see you again one day all the same.

Long live champagne.

Gabrielle

And always with flowers

with a smile . . . a real, real one, from Gatito

And, once again, don't worry, don't let anyone worry.

End of April 1969

Dear Gilberte

Your letter gave me so much pleasure. And it arrived very quickly, which can't be said of mine. The news you gave me was reassuring, because I was worried about Joël. And a little about you too. It's good to know that you're waiting for me, but they don't appear to be in a hurry to get things done so I think patience is necessary. With the help of a colleague's husband, who must be thanked, the problem with the medical commission is almost resolved. And that's one worry less anyway. As for the rest, could I ask you to stop by the garage to make my excuses for not having picked up my car and ask him to keep it a bit longer.

In addition, if I'm not back by the tenth could you take care of my rent? If you are short, you can ask my father, Monsieur Russier. He is up to date on all the problems, but I hesitate to ask him to come for the time being because it's difficult for him to leave my mother all alone.

Finally, and to complete the material details, when you have a moment and if I haven't reappeared, could you send or bring me a package with some things I miss, which will help me endure all this, I'm enclosing the list separately.

Sunday's events produced the effect you can imagine. Yesterday was my birthday but I didn't tell anyone and it passed like the other days, quietly, with a gray sky and this November-like rain. Tomorrow is May 1, a walk in the courtyard—sad solitude—and then the others. Antigone is learning patience, the virtue she lacked above all others. And then, present unhappiness is easier to bear than unhappiness you anticipate or foresee. And as a friend said, "There are better things, but they cost more." The food is hardly any worse than the canteen; as for the rest, it's an eternal subject of meditation and a future subject of conversation.

Tell all those who are worthy of it that I send them my love and I hope to see them again one day. Include Jeanne, whose smile and sense of humor I enjoyed so much, and Huguette, so lively. At first I was struck dumb at finding myself back here. But when you have understood the mechanics . . . That's why I try to be patient, and short of a miracle,[1] I no longer hope for too much, at least not in the near future.

Tell your mother the lilacs will have brought me happiness all the same, and that I'm sure they will flower again. If she knows where I am, I'll write her.

The slave ship gets more and more rotten, but it's still afloat. I'm stopping here, no more space. I send you my love.

With a smile

Gabrielle

[1] But I don't believe in miracles, and perhaps I don't even wish for them.

May 5, 1969

Dear Gilberte

I made up my mind to write you despite the absence of mail because I'm afraid that if you see me again one day—if in spite of everything you see me again—you will be disappointed. I have forced myself to stay in good spirits up till the present, but now I can't go on anymore, for so many reasons I can't go into here. I am just about in the state I was in when I had dinner at your house, except there is no cure here. On the contrary, everything is done to reinforce a depression which had already made its presence felt earlier, and against which I have done nothing but fight for six months until it's made me ill. Human resistance is inexhaustible and yet sometimes I wonder if I'm not going to be completely beyond help after all this. Don't be too upset. Don't mention it. But I don't want you to expect too much of me—in all probability you will have a lot to do helping me get back to the way I used to be.

The people around me are stronger, perhaps it's because they're used to this type of thing, of clinging to values which don't exist for me and which they will find again outside.

And then, at the very bottom of my serenity in the beginning there must have been the idea that despite everything, this could not last because I had done nothing to deserve it, which would be easy to prove.

Now, I have the feeling that once here it's unimportant whether or not you had reasons for coming, it's unimportant whether you're innocent or guilty, you are in a hole, and you go lower and lower. I'm losing my memory of everything. I feel a little as though I were dead. And this letter is also a last effort to try and explain something. I've seen too much, heard too much, I should like to fall into an endless sleep, to forget, but I don't even know if I could. And what hurts me most is that the others find everything normal, what they did before, what they find here, what they'll do again afterward. So much unawareness.

Don't say this to Madame R., tell her it's all right and that I send a kiss to Joël.

Forgive me for writing you so sadly. But it helps to speak to someone. And then afterward, if I'm not too far gone, you'll help me come back to life, won't you?

With love

And a smile—a last little smile,

Gabrielle

May 7, 1969

Dear Gilberte

It's me again because I can't take it anymore. There are times when I feel I'm going to go mad and this is an SOS. I know you can't do anything about it but in desperation I'm writing you all the same, as you would toss a bottle into the sea.

The others around me are resigned, but they know why they are here, while I feel I'm living something out of Kafka. I get through each day by telling myself that it's not possible, that the nightmare is going to end, that they will understand me.

It's not the kind of life here, nor the lack of comforts, nor the supervision that is driving me mad; it's the surroundings, the others. I'm so afraid of being marked forever, of never being able to forget.

I'm trying at all costs to keep my reason, but there are moments, extremely frequent now, when that cracks. I tremble without cause, I imagine all sorts of things, I want to bang my head against the wall.

At the start it was all right because I believed that they must inevitably understand, that my presence here would be one more proof, that they would finally believe. Now I no longer know, everything is mixed up, I don't know what they want anymore. Yet they are kind to me, the nurses too, but their medicines aren't enough, I would give anything for a sleep cure. If only I could forget all this, the degradation, the humiliation, the obscenity. Now I understand the attitude of legal people—if they have people like this before them each day, they can't help but suspect everyone, and see evil everywhere. If I were to stay here for two months I would become like them, I've seen too much already.

Gilberte, forgive me for moaning, I'm frightened, frightened of getting delirious, frightened they'll never believe me. Tell them I wasn't like that, that I respected human beings, that I loved honesty and reason, and that there was nothing suspicious.

I can't go on. I thought I could resist because I had nothing to reproach myself for. But the opposite is true because everything is suspect here, and especially the fact of having done nothing. Because I don't say anything they attribute all kinds of horrors to me, which don't shock but delight them, they are so used to filth they see it everywhere. You might even say they only feel comfortable here, in this environment.

I'm not writing to anyone anymore for fear they will sense that things are not all right, that I'm shaking as I write. Tell Joël I send him a kiss. Don't let him worry too much.

I'm frightened of going mad and especially of not being able to look at people outside anymore without thinking of here, without being disfigured by everything I am seeing.

I'm ashamed of being so low, forgive me. I can't go on. With love

Gabrielle

May 9, 1969

Dear Albert

I can't write at length this evening, I'll do better to-morrow, but I wanted to tell you that I read Nerval. That your cards are so precious to me.

That as long as I am able to write or draw things will be all right. Please send me some felt-tipped pens in all colors (Baignol and Farjon, they don't dry out) and some envelopes. I was sick, but this evening I am able to write, to think, because they gave me some medicine.

The trees are mortally beautiful and in a glass I have a rose, born and living in jail.

Tell me again that I'm not what they think I am here, you can't know. I'm frightened that I shall never forget. Tell me that the sun exists, that truth and purity are of this world, that I wasn't dreaming.

I am so frightened that all this is getting the better of me. The house of the dead.

There are days when I seem slightly dead, others when the torment is so great that I suffocate. But I survive it because of the source.

I'll write you better tomorrow.

Gabrielle

Teorema: Even here, anywhere, leave him his white clothes, his candid integrity. He asked for nothing. God protect him. *F. Mauriac*

But the Green Paradise
The innocent paradise
Is it already farther away than India or China
Can one recall it with plaintive cries
And still animate it with a voice of silver. *Baudelaire*

May 12, 1969

Dear Gilberte

Your letter did me so much good. I haven't received anything for a very long time, and I assume that you haven't received the letters I wrote you either where I asked you to take care of my rent, my car, of Joël, and to send me some laundry. I do hope they forwarded my drawings to Joël all the same, and that he isn't too upset. And perhaps by now you have the letters from the good days, when I was managing to keep on top of things.

They gave me some medicine, I'm better. Don't worry, above all don't worry.

I feel as though I'm in a hole because the world here is so special, and also because I know the real difficulties will begin when I get out. How can I explain it to you— there is a certain sense of security here, you've lost all responsibilities. When I think of what is waiting for me outside I'm afraid, and yet I should so love to see a tree, a real one. That's why being inside is such torment, the thought that I'll have to leave means more torment. Difficult to explain, I shall try later, but certain things are impossible to get across. But don't worry, and tell the others not to worry. Could you send me by mail with the name of the sender written on the outside, a package (small) with

—colored felt-tipped pens
—deodorant and dry shampoo
—a large crochet hook.

And another with wool (there's some at home) and my nylon overall. That way I'll get it faster because packages which are brought are only distributed on Mondays.

It took me a long time to get to know you, Gilberte, you frightened me a little, I didn't dare open up. And then through the days I learned to have confidence and I was at ease with you. You are sensible, upright, and that helped me so much. It's true, you only understand when you love, so I'm going to wait patiently for my lucidity to return. And today I'm pulling myself together as I did the evening when we talked together at length about the SNES. Because I have your letter and it tells me I'm not mad; because you are alive and that'll make me forget what I see here, and what I see is dreadful—it's not tangible but it's in their minds. So many disturbed people —in any case devoted to failure. I'll explain to you. Your dependability, your sense of humor will help me . . . and *Teorema*. Above all that's what I can't stand, what I'm frightened of not being able to forget. Everything is soiled and you know, Jansenist that I am, I can't put up with that. Will I always be fifteen years old? I am incapable of looking at all this with detachment, except when I think that one day I shall get out, but then fresh torment because I don't think I shall be able to stand living as I did these last months, in a comfortable prison continually being spied upon and everything that that means. If I could be sure that everything will be cleared up, I think I would be able to hold out for a long time, a long time. I'm going to try to believe it but I'm afraid of being disillusioned, there's been so much of that already.

Tell your mother, of whom I was very fond, that since I can't get the first rose, I'm sending her a petal from the one that has been helping me to survive for several days.

Tell everyone who deserves it that I'm thinking of them and that, in the stupid way of those whose life slips by them, I am sorry I didn't understand them better, and that the red tortoise is moving forward shakily, but it is moving forward, if it falls down it will get up again.

With love

Gabrielle

[TO HER PARENTS]   *May 13, 1969*

In this so special world which you can only understand if you have lived in it, I try to roll myself into a ball, to see nothing, to hear nothing. I look at my syringa blossom and the sky outside, a little pale, a little sad. Spring has not really come back this year, and the approaching summer will without doubt lack the brightness of the summers that went before. I try not to think of the future, to live from day to day.

Marseilles is a rotten town. And yet I loved Provence so much. I loved Marseilles too, sparkling in the night, and the Estaque, and the boat, on which we had set our sights, sleeping in the port. It was called *The Misunderstood.*

So much has happened since that day in May when you left St. Charles Station, papa. Everything had been in the works for some months even then, but nothing had been said. Each of us thought he was dreaming. So many things, so many friends. It would fill several books. But then, at least this will serve to measure the strength and price of friendship, when it is true. And we shall try to forget the others, the wolves.

I don't regret anything except having dragged so many people into what appears today to be a disaster. Tell me you know "that you only see clearly with your heart," that we are now in the black hole of appearances and ugliness, but that truth, in its simplicity, will return with the sun. Tell me that you aren't too sad. For such a long time we have lived with the barrier of space between us. And yet, since February '58, eleven years ago already, we have always been together. I am with you—not in sadness and misery—I should like you to have the calm I feel at this moment, to tell you I'm waiting for you, and that nothing can happen to us. With a smile

And love

Gabrielle

[TO HER PARENTS] *May 13, 1969*

The atmosphere here is as you would imagine. The guardian angels are kind, but the company pretty awful. I'm all right in my cell and leave it as little as possible. The best moments are with the choir and at mass. The chaplain is a Dominican, like the sisters who come to visit us and who are marvels of serenity and understanding. I hope I shall be able to pay them a visit afterward at Saint Zachary where they live.

Saint Zachary, those were the good times of our walks together when we were discovering Provence. I am going to try and be strong so that those times will come again, so that we shall find Saint Victoria again just as it is turning mauve, so that we can pick everlasting flowers.

Since I live partly in the company of Baudelaire and Rimbaud and partly with the rabble, I don't really know where I am. I can no longer tell if what I'm writing is lucid, reasonable.

But I should like to be able to say to you, as before,
till tomorow
till always
I send you my love

Gabrielle

May 15, 1969

Dear Albert

I write to you without even knowing if you receive my letters. I have been alone in a cell since yesterday; you have no idea how much better I am. The girl who went away, whom I am replacing, left some little objects, thinking of the one who would come next, without knowing who it would be, little nothings, some paint boxes, a bunch of ferns, a little washing powder in a jar. Little nothings, but it's the first time since I've been here that I have seen true solidarity between prisoners—true and spontaneous. And then nothing = everything here. Since I've been downstairs, I see less sky, but I am so very much freer that the little morsel of cloud which floats by has a marvelous denseness. In the evening when they are all outside talking to each other, I am alone with all of you and I am sure Mozart is not sad, that you are listening to him for me and he is not sad.

For the first time I have become a little like the person you knew; I washed the walls with the spoils of fortune, I set up house, and I decorated: a card from Claudette, the Miró, and two pictures a girl left me . . . a black shawl on the bed. For the time being I've rediscovered my vitality in my snail's shell, my refuge. Before I dreamed; I read without taking in too much of what I was reading; I rolled myself into a ball in a corner, like the cats, trying not to think, not to hear; but a sort of endless torment held me like a vise, I trembled without reason. I couldn't write. Only letters but with so much difficulty.

Now it seems to me that it could be different (but I have hardly any paper), send me a large-format spiral-bound notebook and a felt-tipped Tempo pen. Send them because packages which are brought are only distributed on Monday. Put the name of the sender on it, send some stamps too. I have received nothing except two cards up till now. I have Rimbaud and Baudelaire with me. I shall never be able to tell you how true they are. Especially Baudelaire. Rimbaud is another story, another kind of truth, the experience of a parallel world that many are searching for here, I mean were searching for, before coming here (you see I'm getting muddled), they believe real life is missing. But these are the untainted ones. The only ones in this astonishing and traumatizing universe. The pure lines of Milan are far away, but I still see all the greens of Pasolini's countryside, and the golds of the church; at Pisa I laughed, I lost my temper with the tourists, perhaps you were ashamed to be with a mad-woman. The cypress at the convent of Fra Angelico.

"Provence is a cemetery / Delivered, I shall sleep there /
In the shade of the cypresses."

At the moment the night is the color of night. Tender. The syringa slowly wilts. Roots of my childhood, where have you gone?

Gone to the wood to gather ferns, meadow saffron, and jonquils.

The lovely wood where the hawthorn smiles, the river from Guermantes will never cease to flow across the plains. "The scent of the invisible and persistent lilacs." I'm stopping here because my censors will think I'm writing you in code, and you'll think I'm going mad and that I miss Proust too much.

Mouse, mouse, Frotadou sends you a hearty kick.

P.S: If in the course of your wanderings you find a house in the country, in the quiet, keep it so that I can go to rest there after the Hôtellerie des Baumettes cure.

"The roses of electricity open again
In the garden of my memory."   Apollinaire
                                               Gabrielle

May 16, 1969

Dear R. J.

I imagine that you have been wandering all over Europe and that you have returned satisfied with your grand tour. I haven't forgotten our plan to have dinner at L'Estaque, you know, but I've "moved house" since the last time we saw each other, and in spite of myself I won't be able to realize that old dream for the time being. I am billeted here in the Hôtellerie des Baumettes, for the same reasons as before, but on grounds that I don't understand. The sojourn will have been much longer this time and is getting longer still.

There are highs and lows, particularly lows, but now things are OK. The solitude at least. The possibility of shutting oneself into the "outside" world—if I can put it that way—of keeping in close touch with one's memories, with oneself. "Rest" after a Baudelaire-like despair. It was a miserable, agonizing crossing of the Acheron with doomed women as galley companions. But in the last three days I have discovered a relative freedom in my solitude. At the same time *la Vive* has found again a little of the vital élan, a little of that spark, of that energy, which have made what many people wanted to see in her—the heroine of a book.

Everything started four years ago, as you know so well, and the other day, in the sunshine on the Cours Mirabeau, you said that everything had changed, fashions, types of literature. But I knew that nothing had changed, only the appearances. The essence is elsewhere, in the "spheres of intensity." The other day the priest here told me that I'm like Dreyer's Joan of Arc. That reminded me of many things. I like the chaplain very much. Perhaps you would laugh to see me sing in the choir. But I enjoy going there, to sing with the others, to try, even here, to make others "happy." Of course, from the outside, it may seem peculiar. I'll tell you about it. There are sisters who come too,

Dominicans. They have told me to think of myself as a "political prisoner." It isn't easy. But in fact they are so right.

I would have so much to say to you. If I survive all this I shall try to tell you about it for your future books. Not about this experience, because I think I'm beginning to climb back up the slope a little, but about everything that was insidious, corrosive, what went before, what will follow. The book by Cocteau—I read it again, it's simple, it's straightforward, it all happens in three days. How lucky theater people are.

The character in a novel takes longer to reach the end of his destiny, he is doing it all the time, it's hard, mortally painful: Sisyphus.

I remember the seminar at the institute for foreign students, the floral armchair. The wife of an executive who was reliving her adolescence. *L'Avventura*. I remember it without nostalgia because that was yesterday, and it will be tomorrow too. "The immutable does not live within your walls, the immutable lives within you, slow man, continual man." I know you don't believe it anymore, or you appear not to. It is to prove that that I am here, and the sisters are right. Thanks to a "talk" I've learned how to love language, flowers, and even people again. You won't get much pride out of it but Pygmalion . . . It seems to me that that was worth writing. Of being given life.

Best Wishes

Gabrielle

May 16, 1969

Dear old Michel*

I hope that the last week of your vacation went off well. At the time when you must have been traveling, I came to vacation here, where I have been living since April 25. I did not write you before so as not to upset you, but I am doing so now because I guess you will have been brought up to date if you went to see Joël. Moreover, I don't know when you will receive this letter, the mail seems to be held up somewhere and for my part I receive virtually nothing.

Above all don't worry about me, although I have not received the packages I requested, I'm not bad, and for the rest I have done nothing to justify my presence here. My father's attorney will confirm this to you by telephone if you want to be reassured, or my Marseillais attorney, Monsieur Raymond Guy. If you have time, send me some postcards so I can decorate my cell a bit. For the last two days I have been alone and my morale is better than before, I am trying to organize myself, to work. The impatient nature you once knew is learning patience.

I'm writing you because I'm worried about the children. Joël is in the same place he was during the Easter vacation. I write to him but I don't know if he gets my letters. If you have a moment, go and say hello to him and above all reassure him because I'm certain he understood that I was coming here.

I have also written Valérie, but since she knows absolutely nothing I talk to her about the rain and good

* Her ex-husband.

weather. I hope she doesn't notice that my letters do not correspond with hers. They are kind enough here not to put the "censored" stamp on what I write her (the sisters open the mail in Savoy). Write her. She gets back the 10th or 11th, if I haven't gotten out (you never do know when you're getting out of here) someone must go and fetch her at the station. You could find out the date of her return by telephoning the Social Security Department Camps Service at the beginning of June. I think that Madame R. will agree to take her with Joël. You could then pay Madame R. (against receipt) for the whole of June; she is not rich and I was only able to give her 100 francs when I left.

I interrupted myself because I just received my first package—some wool, some Scotch tape, a little laundry, a drawing I liked—life is beautiful.

They've been giving me a hard time for months, they are trying to wear me down, but although I'm fading little by little, I don't think they will ever stop me from experiencing the joy that one discovers in little things— a flower, a smile, an occasional silence.

We have shared good and bad times before. Don't be too angry with me for making you share bad times again. *Don't worry.* Take care of Joël, send cards to Valérie (packages are not allowed). You'll see, a day will come when we can smile with them once more, for real this time. I relish the idea of having a drink at Le Grillon with you. I'll put on a dress in your honor, you won't have to drag an androgynous hippie to the Cours Mirabeau.

Bise[1]

Gabrielle

¹ The bise is a warm little wind which blows from the Gobi Desert, it fights against the storm . . . and it will win.

Friday, May 16, 1969

Dear Gilberte

I'm writing you again, as you have permitted, although I haven't received anything from you. There is one sign that Saint Antoine exists—I just received the second package I asked for (there's absolutely no trace of the first) and I thank whoever sent or brought it.

Life had already picked up: I have been alone in a cell for two days, and feel so much better in my solitude. Yesterday I came back to life a bit, I moved the furniture, cleaned the walls, organized my refuge. And now I have my parcel, a clean dress, the picture by Luc on the wall, my own little corner. I'm OK, ready to hold out for a long time. Tell those who deserve it at the lycée not to worry. I hope too that you, Gilberte, have not had too many problems because of me, materially or spiritually. I know from experience that it's harder for those who are outside than for those inside. But your sense of humor, your determined spirit, will stop you, I'm sure, from following my tracks down the road to depression. Above all I do hope my disappearance has not affected your mother's morale too deeply. Tell her I send her a kiss, that I think of her, that I try to be like her by always keeping myself neat and clean (that's not always easy here) and leading my life with care and attention to detail, by trying to chase away depression when it sneaks up on me. And I value my good fortune at being able to write and read. But I would very much like not to be able to hear anymore because these ladies, my coprisoners, have conversations (through the windows) that I won't forget for a long while.

I shall at least have learned to do each act slowly, patiently, and God knows, if indeed there is a God, that was not my wont.

In short, a little life in slow motion, that won't do any harm. But unfortunately I imagine that now, as I begin to part with my earlier illusions, they will start making me come out of my shell.

I can visualize the little red shoes and our first conversation last year, going down toward St. Louis for a coffee. I was very, very intimidated. Now you mean a lot to me —and it's not because I am in prison. But perhaps it is because I'm in prison that I dare tell you.

And then, it has always seemed to me that I don't deserve people looking after me. At the moment I accept it—make a virtue of necessity—but afterward . . .

Afterward I think I shall take up the bag I came with and go lose myself in the crowd, or beside the water. I have learned to do without everything or nearly, I have also learned not to take on responsibilities anymore since I collapsed under their weight. And since I don't know how to steer a middle course . . . That's the danger here —the shock of getting out. Learning to live again. I shall want to walk, walk without a destination, without money, without anything. To lose myself, to disappear, I'm frightened of the day when they will uproot me from this world where, when all is said and done, we are protected. Especially now that I am alone; the convent, the "rest." Difficult not to say "I" all the time. Because "outside" is a more and more diffuse memory—sometimes painfully nostalgic—that one drives away so as not to be hurt by it. However, I should like to continue to write you because I find that writing for oneself is—I don't know—absolutely absurd. Even if I'm aware that sending these epistles is absurd too.

I shall try not to "run away" when I get out. So that this experience will at least make some sense for those who come after me. But the temptation will be great.

Thank you for being there. For helping me not to forget that the earth exists. My love to everyone. Tell them that the lycée coffee was good! Tell them too that true fidelity is that of ideas. And that is why I'm here.

With love

Gabrielle

May 19, 1969

Dear Gilberte

I received your "fifth" letter today. It was the third for me and took nearly eight days to reach me. For my part, I have written you often, but apparently nothing has arrived.

Appearances to the contrary, however, I don't think our discussion has been falling on deaf ears. Everything is coming apart, but the essence has not been touched. The news is—slight, and occasionally I get worried about material matters, about Joël too. But it's so important for me to know that you are there, at Saint Antoine, that you were able to reassure my parents. Your letters bring me a breath of air from the outside, stop me from forgetting that somewhere there is a home which used to be mine, a school I grumbled about when I had to leave in the morning, but which I liked very much, and teachers with whom, little by little, I became friendly. Tell them softly that things are all right. That I thank them for thinking of me, that it helps me to know they do—a lot. Don't overlook Claudette's teacher. I now know it was you who went out of your way with the package. A sad walk for you no doubt. When you aren't used to them, these walls are terrible. But the things you brought help me to live here—especially all the drawings. I put the picture on the wall, and I dream. I also crochet a lot. Two things I was hardly in the habit of doing. I try not to think of the past too much—my memories hurt me—nor of the future because I'm terribly apprehensive about it. To survive. If there were not all this painful past and uncertain future I would be calmer. So I'm trying to forget, to forget everything, and at the same time I know I must not, that I must write you, that I must keep a tie with the outside world. I envy the people who are "redeeming their sins" as they say, who are here for something and who will find freedom afterward, when they leave. At least they have a reason to wait.

I don't really have one. To leave one nightmare to enter into another. Having come here for nothing, gratuitously, to leave for the same reason. I am trying to make myself forget the bitterness, but there is discouragement along with the patience, because I no longer even hope that it will all be cleared up. I have no more desire to return to Saint Antoine, or anywhere else, that's what frightens me. Perhaps that will get better. But when I do get out you will all be so tired. I realize that it's hard for you too, I'm mad at myself for inflicting all this on you indirectly —even if the responsible parties are elsewhere. I shall have exhausted and upset you.

I should have written you something gayer. Don't get worried. Wait for me, I shall try to come back, to listen to the doctor. But now I have fallen into the hole, into emptiness, I don't know if I shall know how to climb back out. In order to get better, you have to want to—and to have reasons. It seems to me that I no longer do. Everything I loved has been spoiled. Dirtied.

With love

Gabrielle

[TO HER PARENTS]   *May 27, 1969*

Don't be upset, I have little mail and no visitors, but I know it must be as hard for you all to know that I'm here, and I don't want all this to wear you down. Think, as I do when I'm in a good frame of mind, that great joy is well worth great suffering. Here I am surrounded by people who have for the most part ruined their lives for money. Perhaps you were too successful in teaching me that money has absolutely no importance in relation to real values. It is always this way when I am calm, like this evening, I believe very strongly, and I would so much like you to feel it with me, that, hard as it may be, this must not leave a mark on us, because it isn't real. Perhaps they will never want to believe me—and I so often revolt against the idea of being incarcerated for nothing—but the important thing is to bear the truth within oneself. It was, it is so simple. So simple that no one can see it. Like all beautiful and simple things.

Wait for me patiently, like poor Frotadou who is so "brave," and who looks so astonished and candid that when they took me away, one sympathetic "policeman" worried about what would become of him.

Wait for me, I shall come back, not too destroyed, I hope. And if I am too destroyed, I shall try tenderly to become again

your Gabrielle

May 28, 1969

Dear Michel

Monsieur Guy told me that you had telephoned him. I am so pleased you are taking care of Joël. Thank you for having suggested it spontaneously. I was so worried about him, he saw the people arriving to take me away, and about Valérie who was so happy in Savoy, and who was surely coming back with the idea that she would try hard, that I would be less tired, and that everything would be all right.

The end of this despair is no longer in sight, everything is mixed up in my head because I see and hear the kind of things around me that I was never able to bear. Materially it's not bad, it's psychologically that it's hard. The others look as if they are all right, they even seem to enjoy themselves. They outdo each other boasting of their crimes.

Perhaps I'm writing improper, and therefore censorable things. So I'll just say that the drink we're going to have together at Le Grillon seems further and further away to me, more and more unlikely, because in spite of monumental resistance, they're going to succeed in driving me completely out of my mind. Already I can't read anymore because everything makes me think about things that are over and done with, I agonize, I hark back, I never stop asking myself what I'm doing here, why they are letting me plunge deeper and deeper into a prison worse than prison itself, that of torment, of doubt, of envy, by screaming against the wall of incomprehension, against the absurdity, by letting myself go, by "resigning myself," or by giving up the right to remain my lucid and rational self. I can't take any more of living with people whose corruption becomes more obvious with each passing day. Only the guards help me to get by a little. I no longer even believe in a peaceful future. I no longer believe in anything.

So if all this takes too much out of me, if I never find my old smile again, I beg you, help Joël and Valérie to grow up, to be strong, and if possible shield them from what we have discovered each in our own way.

I don't really know what I'm writing anymore. I can't

stop thinking and everything is jumbled up in my head.

Look after them—as you are able. You know how angry I am with myself for not being able to do it.

I have confidence in you. You had changed so much. I only wanted to say thank you and here I send you two incoherent pages.

Best

G

Dear Michel

Both at the same time I received your letter of May 20 and that of the 12th containing a card from Valérie which distresses me; she says she has not had news of me; now I wrote her every week, sending her pictures. Like you I think that she is fragile, so I wrote yesterday to my colleague and neighbor who will take care of them, I hope. Everything you say in your letter is so true. You can't know how pleased I was to receive it and I am so worried about Joël and Valérie. It was only the day before yesterday that I had news of them. The mail is all mixed up, month-old letters arrive together with others that are two weeks old, and I no longer know how to write, all the same I should like to try and say to you, to tell you that I have done nothing to justify my presence here, that your card made me so *happy* that for the first time since I've been here I burst into tears, that I'm frightened for the kids, especially now that Valérie has come back or is about to come back. She won't understand. I wanted you to know also that if my friends have been a bit suspicious it's because they don't know you, I'm sure they have confidence in you now, that they no longer have doubts about you. I didn't talk about you to them because that too would have been difficult to make them understand; the kind of balance we had found after the storm is so rare and it was turning into total mutual confidence and respect.

But I remember that some of them were beginning to understand.

I hadn't told Joël to keep the secret. He must have thought it better to do so, he saw the people who took me away. I don't know how that kid manages to be so strong. I'm afraid he'll crack. And neither do I know what you can say to Valérie, I trust you. But it's sad, she's been so much better since she has been at Cruet, she wrote such pretty letters, so balanced. I thought she would forget this black year. I wanted to think of you all happy, as you said, I try but I'm frightened all the time, frightened of not being able to look after them anymore, frightened for their smiles. Michel, you know how to find strength in difficult situations, I remember St. Tropez. I'm forcing myself to write, it's hard, not only because I imagine that I shall be read twice over, but also because I'm at the end of my rope. I'm making myself do it all the same because I'm trying not to surrender, not to forget that you all exist, that the world is not as it is here. I try desperately to convince myself that I'm here by "accident" as those who guard us say, but because I'm going round in circles I can't read anymore. To think, that really is becoming an accident but now I should prefer the hospital because by battling against absurdity one goes mad, an accident rights itself, I don't know anymore, I'm slowly losing my grip on things, I'm too scared of being incurable.

Thank you for being you.

Best

Gabrielle

Friday, May 30, 1969

Dear Gilberte

If you can take care of the children, I hope my husband will help you. Would you tell them at the lycée that I was very fond of them.

Don't be mad at me, I'm exhausted because my lucidity and understanding of things and people will have served for nothing. They keep telling me through the papers I receive that I'm guilty, and I'm beginning to envy those who really are and who laugh in the courtyard. I shall never be able to laugh again, they've made a mountain out of a molehill. They are keeping me here for some things I did a very long time ago, not in the least bit reprehensible so I don't understand. I keep turning the blackest thoughts over and over in my mind. I no longer know how to reason, to think.

I'm frightened for the children

I'm so frightened

they only had me. They were so used to knowing I was there, always, faithfully, even if I was sad, even if I was depressed.

Protect them. I know. I'm asking a lot of you, you have

your own troubles, your work. Protect them. I don't even know if I shall be able to write them again as before.

I thought so highly of you, I liked you so much.

help me, I'm exhausted

I'm frightened that the children will be upset. I no longer know who I can trust them to.

Help me if you still can, I no longer believe in anything, in anyone, but I don't want Joël and Valérie to cry, they've been unhappy enough as it is.

You will have to lie a bit to them. Only to them. Don't believe what people tell you, the lawyer's hopes, perhaps it's not his fault but he's not going to win because they're being so vicious. I don't know, I don't understand. Everyone lies to me to make me hold on but it no longer has any effect on me. I must forget that I've had another life. I must become like the others here, they don't give a damn, they're all right in their network of lies and their mediocrity.

But I can't take any more. I've tried, I can't. Gilberte, tell those who understand, who are able to understand, that it is better to die in a real way than like this, in this dunghill.

I try to tell myself that it's less serious than an accident, the hospital, and yet to become incapable of reasoning is worse.

It's not working out.

I don't even know how to sign off anymore.

A nothing, a limp rag, and Saint Antoine is dead.

G

Friday, May 30, 1969

I'm still writing. I wanted to try to reassure you all but now I think it's impossible. You were wrong when you told me that truth grows in the shadow of prisons. They are keeping me here for motives I don't understand, that have nothing to do with reality, and I can't go on not understanding. I envy the girls who know what they've done, what they are being held responsible for. I don't know, perhaps their conversations are making me stupid, crazy, dizzy. Albert, I'm at the end of my rope because they're getting the better of me. I no longer know where truth and justice lie because I'm being pervaded by the atmosphere, because I receive papers of which I understand nothing. Is it really not possible to end this massacre. Slowly, insidiously, the attempt on my life is reaching a climax. I don't know how it can be possible but it is. I would have preferred being beaten a hundred times—or dying violently. At the moment I regret I did not do what I was so tempted to do one day on the way to Aix: to drive across that barrier, I don't know what it's called anymore, that's in the middle of the expressway.

I can no longer be strong, or patient, because I have no reason to be. I can't even smile anymore, or read three lines, everything gets jumbled up all the time. I ask myself why they keep me here, why they tell me I'm guilty, I would so much like to understand what I'm guilty of. Tell them to stop this massacre, I beg you. I know it won't do any good, but I'm asking all the same, if they wanted to hurt me . . . I didn't want to [*sic*] as they well know. I'm so weary of this world where there's nothing but madwomen, I'd much rather be in a lunatic asylum, anything would be better than their gossip, their meanness. I keep shut up inside myself as much as possible, but inside things go round and round in my head, I can't stop thinking. They at least are unaware, that's their strength. Real toughs, all of them. You might even say that they enjoy themselves here. But then they don't think. I do nothing but that. Tell me that this nightmare is going to end; the guards here kindly tell me it is, but I don't believe in anyone anymore. Tell me all the same, too bad if it isn't true. And yet I have obeyed them, I have tried so hard to obey them, so what do they want. That I go completely nuts? It won't take long. I'm not saying this to frighten you, to hurt you, I'm saying it so that you will forgive me if you no longer recognize me.

Look after Joël and Valérie with Michel. If I couldn't then, I won't be able to now, I'm finished. Albert, this must be an illness but that's the way it is, I've had more than enough of them giving me a hard time for nothing, I should like to sleep, to forget.

Good-bye, I don't know when I'll see you again, I just don't know.

Gabrielle

[TO RAYMOND JEAN] *June 5, 1969*

Your letter of the 25 received yesterday. Too late now, nothing can make me smile. I should still like to be able to tell you that I wasn't looking elsewhere.

But the experience thing ended a long while ago.

But I destroyed what was suffocating me. For a year I had tried to survive.

I don't know anymore.

At least I should like to think that what is happening to me will be of use to other people. The SNES at Aix wanted to see you, D. told me. Do it for the principle of the thing. Out of republican uprightness.

And too, if you would like to, in memory of Claude Simon.

In memory of Chloë.

I am at the point where I would like all this to end tomorrow morning like in *L'étranger*, but that's impossible here. It is absurdity without end. I have been crushed by the rock. It got too heavy for me.

Forget me, I'm no longer myself. I don't think I shall ever be again. Write books.

Gabrielle

[TO MADAME GILBERTE T.]   *June 24, 1969*

I say all sorts of things to you, I keep you from going to sleep—always. And then remorse. And worst of all, I never dare tell you the most important thing. Well, since lined paper doesn't exist anymore, since the dreadful Minos no longer risks meningitis trying to interpret my remarks (badly)

Too bad

I'm writing to say

that you are the first to have succeeded in making me smile. Obviously this doesn't show since you are the first. But it's true—I swear—Frotadou's honor.

that it's lovely, better than that, to be with you because here at last is someone balanced, who understands without dramatizing, with a smile.

Someone reassuring, in short precisely what I should find on my path at the end of June to teach me how to walk again. Someone reassuring, that's very important now and then. No kidding, I mean it seriously.

And then too I don't know how to say thank you. I only know how to think it, so I'll say it in Italian—*grazie*.

It was brave to bring wool to someone whose erratic reasoning worried and upset you. And you were extremely indulgent to have offered me Châteauneuf du Pape instead of a reproach.

Mea culpa. Will I ever be able to repent. I should only like to be able to now, to make us both forget that long month of May.

I think I shall be able to, thanks to the smile.

I shall be able to. And to walk too. And they will all be most surprised that Thouvenette has succeeded in bringing off this little miracle.

Do I have the right, although there are no more bars, or prisons, or walls, to tell you that I am very fond of you and that I send you my love.

Gabrielle

July 16

Dear Gilberte

That horrible prosecutor (the district attorney) has appealed.

Everything will have to begin all over again.

I have no more confidence. Monsieur Guy is content with hugging me. After dreadful vacillations I am going to leave for the Pyrenees to escape the depression which follows a sleep cure. The mail will be forwarded. I receive letters from strangers who are fascinated by this story.

Will I be able to thank you enough. I'm blocked, paralyzed by psychoanalysis, I don't even dare say thank you to you, or to tell you that you've been a sister to me because that too is suspect. I shall also have to overcome this form of depression, to take things as they are.

Look at Italy, it is so beautiful. And the lake of Como because of Fabrice del Dongo, the cypresses, the time when they fought healthily—with swords.

You have earned the right a hundred times over to enjoy the sky and the trees, Serviers, good Jeanne, and the energetic Huguette in peace.

Auguri, tanti auguri to your trio.

Tell your mother that I owe the fact I am still up and about to her, to her too, that I didn't write because I had too many problems. Give her my love, and tell her I shall send her a little air from the Pyrenees.

And so many other things as well.

Gabrielle

If I don't leave any keys for the cleaning woman because of the cat, I shall put a double set in your box, you never know.

Thursday, end of July, 1969

Dear Michel

I'm going away to rest up in the Pyrenees, hoping that this will spare me a sleep cure.

Joël's coming back on August 30 around 6:30. He will have to be fetched and put in the Palette until school starts.

Until my return, beginning of September.

If you can go and see him he will be happy. For the time being he thinks the battle's been won.

I receive piles of letters from strangers, from left and right, which uphold me and condemn my treatment. They too think it's over with. Fortunately, because I fear their indignation is harmful to me.

I'm scared that Aix and a press campaign, with which they hope to help me, may prejudice my case. The R.s are out of town so now the representatives of society are mad at me.

Only one tactic—to reduce the story to what it was, that is to say, nothing. Not to fall into the trap that everyone is holding out to me by trying to help; the suggestions from the left—philosophy, psychoanalysis; the suggestions from the right—divorce, etc.

Above all, when you get home, don't go shouting at anyone.

The only thing that can save us from now on is

—that you take care of the children

—that you remain calm (everyone's in a state) and perhaps that you come to the trial to say that I was "highly moral" and that you still respect me. Perhaps my father will send a new attorney.

My story is getting the whole world excited. It must be cut down to size, deglamorized. Don't talk of anything, be calm.

Bise

Gabrielle

Rest, we shall need all our strength. Tell Valérie that I send her lots and lots of love.

La Recouvrance
Wednesday, July 23

Dear Gilberte

I guess you will have read *L'Observateur* since Hug... is a subscriber; everything's in there, even details... hearing. And above all—I shall be torn insid... cause it was the Public Minister E. N. who... alarm to the judge, who put the prosecut... I'm trying to rest, but I live in tormen... will be no more treatment. Little r... have to sell off the apartment, f... somewhere, put the kids in a... while waiting to find work. r... ation itself is dramatic. F...

down, I have little strength for writing, but above all I have to watch the stamps, I'm living off nothing surrounded by wealthy people. The *maison de repos* is full of people who have undergone sleep cures, not much fun. But the owners are charming. The wife is a sociology teacher. She seems to have a lot of contacts, is going to try to get in touch with the minister. I'm forcing myself to hold on, so that I shall see you again one day, but I'm tired, I keep thinking, I don't sleep anymore.

As I was going away I was too sad to leave Frotadou mewing on the stairs. I asked Madame R. to keep him until you could take him to Serviers. I hope you won't be mad at me, and that you will find a farm for him where he will be happy. If it is difficult, leave him in the country. In any case he will be less unhappy than at the Résidence Nord. I shall not be able to pay you back for everything you've done for me for ages. Perhaps only with a lot of affection.

I shall force myself not to go completely off the rails, completely nuts. They are trying to rid me of my guilt ᵈe.

eveʰall force myself because I have discovered you and now I leave the Résidence, I shan't let you go. From luck foᵘ have a semi basket case on your hands. Worse Thereᵐy dear, you're a mother cat too.

they seemᵉs here, a farm, and lots of nutty people— chological pᵉazy than me—but they only have psy- When youʳ no real difficulties.

want me to repʰ ᵉ at Serviers, write me. And if you and soon I'll be ᵇ ᵉ a stamp. I am absolutely broke, ᵗ the street. By the way, what

would you think of an appeal for help in *L'Observateur?*
I'm not kidding.

A girl has put Mozart on the phonograph, it's sad to
realize you'll never be able to treat yourself to an hour
of Mozart again.

I hope you made the best of your stay.

Once again, tell your mother I send my love. Best
wishes to Huguette and Jeanne. I forgot to tell the latter
that she was wearing a very pretty green dress the other
evening.

Your

Gabrielle

Who is trying to forget her first name.

La Recouvrance
August 1, 1969

Dear Michel

I'm sending you this letter as one would throw a bottle
into the ocean, without knowing if I shall see you again
very soon or never. I'm so tormented about the future I
can't rest, or read, or write. And they no longer really
know what to do with me here. If I have to go into a
clinic, I would prefer Marseilles. I'm going to try to explain to you but it's so complicated. As for the trial, we
don't know if it was the public prosecutor who got mad at
the tribunal's decision, or if it came from higher up. There
have been masses of contradictory articles in the press. My

father has engaged a big lawyer . . . as far as that's concerned we can relax and pray.

But the situation is very serious for me, for the children, because I'm washed up as far as the Ministry of National Education is concerned (which might have happened even if I had been acquitted). I shall have just enough to live for six months because of the taxes, legal fees, rent, etc. In addition, the ministry has landed me in an impossible situation because they have just deducted the month and a half's salary for the time I was at Les Baumettes which at the same time makes me forfeit my right to social security. I'm trying to explain to you but it's even more complicated than that. I should just like to tell you that I'm so afraid for the children; that it's not my fault the trial got out of hand, everyone said so; that I'm incapable of working, I no longer understand anything I hear, or read. I am utterly ruined intellectually and physically and I so much want the children to survive and escape all this. If something happens to me and you need laundry for them, the keys are with Madame R. (I have resigned myself to leaving them there). Robert sent me their photos, Valérie is very beautiful, I'm going to try to write her but I can't do it. I am so desperate: How can I tell you that the weather is beautiful, that the sun exists?

If there is not much left at home it's because since the ghastly Baumettes experience everything's been set adrift. I'm counting on you for the children's sake. I didn't want to worry you with all these stories, not to hurt you, but they need you now that I'm no longer good for anything.

Joël wrote me, he would like to have some stamped

envelopes if you could send him some; I have to go to Trabes to get them, take a cab, etc. . . . I don't have the strength, or the money.

I only have the strength to go back to Marseilles and perhaps to call on you for help.

You can't know the effort it's costing me to write you, I should so like to explain to you, I can't. I'm lost among the contradictory signs which are coming from all sides. I can't go on, Michel.

I send you my love, desperately

Gabrielle

La Recouvrance
August 27, 1969

Dear Gilberte

Don't be too mad at me; if I haven't written you it's because I was lower than rock bottom, paralyzed by the torment, incapable of writing or reading.

In the last two days I have managed to write a little, and today I got your letter. Perhaps you would be less cross with me if I told you that I have written to no one since the beginning of my stay here at La Recouvrance. First of all because the torment started again as soon as I thought of taking up my pen, next because each day I told myself that I wouldn't last here, that I would leave for Marseilles. At one point I all but called for help, for someone to come and fetch me. In the end they succeeded in keeping me here, but I have just decided to leave the day after tomorrow, come what may. I did a mini sleep cure at Lannemezan hospital, where the psychiatrist announced my condition was completely justified after everything that had happened to me, and that I would not recover my equilibrium until after the trial.

So I shall be in Marseilles on Sunday, and my aunt will join me on Thursday. I don't know what will happen next. The appeal does not take place until the 15th. I hope you will be free to accompany me on that fateful day as you did last time. I hope too that I'm not a burden to you, who have done so much, and that you don't consider me too ungrateful. I'm totally "blocked" at the moment, you would think that I have no interest in other people. And yet it's not so. Deep down inside me there's a Gabrielle who is very fond of you, of you and your mother, but who no longer knows how to say it.

Thank you for having taken care of Frotadou. Would you tell Jeanne and Huguette when you write them that I send them my love. Still so much to say to you (and in a muddle): the hope that I'll see you again, that I won't leave Marseilles this year, that I'll become my old self again, that I'll find my intelligence and lucidity again. Everything is mixed up in my head, I can't concentrate anymore. To put it simply, I'm going to try to hold on, to make an ultimate effort to get out of the woods, because of all of you, the people I loved.

But I'm not a pretty sight, and you must expect to find a limp washrag on your return.

I'm thinking of you down there in Tremonzey, I hope you have succeeded in forgetting the problems I have given you, that the Napoleonic code has given us at least.

I shall be happy to see you again, you're so dependable.

I send my love to you and your mother too. Tell her her help has allowed us to win a battle and that it will help us to win the war; that I am thinking of her, that I shall think of her.

Best

Gabrielle

La Recouvrance
August 29, 1969

Dear Michel

Don't be mad at me for not writing you for such a long time; I have been very ill, and paralyzed by the idea of taking up a pen. Besides, I haven't written to anyone during my stay here except the children.

Today, I am able to pick up the pen, although my thoughts are all confused.

I have not exactly recouped my strength here, I look like a walking corpse. But I'm going to do everything I can to "hold out" until the appeal, alone at first, then with the children, if there is an improvement.

I am happy about Valérie who sent me a very good letter. I shall go and see her and Joël at La Palette. If you would take me there one day (I don't think I'm able to drive).

My aunt gets to Marseilles on Thursday the fourth, I shall be there a little before, despite the inconveniences of solitude, because I have made an enormous effort to remain here but now I can't go on.

I hope we won't quarrel anymore when I get back and that you will help me have patience to bear the pain and depression until the trial. The doctors all agree in thinking that my state is quite normal taking into account what has happened to me in the last year.

I also wanted to thank you for the letter that you did for my father. He told me about it and appears to think it is very useful. Need I tell you once again that I would like this nightmare to end so that we could all be together again, all four of us as we were before, with our little difficulties which were nothing beside what is waiting for us. I say us, because if my state doesn't improve, you will have to take care of the children.

For the moment I am going to try to live from day to day, to have patience; but I mustn't have any illusions, I am no better than I was in July, probably worse—of course the situation is worse too.

I am rereading your letter of August 6. Everything that you say to me is good—and reasonable and encouraging.

You're right about the National Education. But what worries me is that I have lost a lot of my intellectual faculties, not to mention my more or less ruined physical state, in consequence I shall not be able to find other work for quite a while to come. Above all I am going to try to put a good face on it for the children, even if I don't take them with me right away, so that they won't be too "shocked." But that will be hard. I go around looking so funereal here, the other women's bantering doesn't succeed in cheering me up. They are much less ill than I, but then they haven't been through the difficulties I have.

It's taken a lot of patience for me to stay here, and often I've wanted to ask you to help. But in the end I held on, and I hope that I shall keep holding on. I shall write to Madame C., who sent me a wonderful letter. I send you my love, hoping I'll see you soon, that all this will die down and that you weren't wrong to have confidence in me.

Gabrielle